Praise for *SVG Animations*

Few people are as passionate about animation on the web as Sarah, and her new book is a treasure trove of knowledge. If you want to animate SVG on the web, you simply must read this book.

—*Jack Doyle, GreenSock*

"I find Sarah Drasner's animations a delight to see—expressive, fluid, and graceful. But not only is she a superb animator, she can also explain exactly why and how to use the tools at your disposal to create the animations you desire. Her cogent and lucid prose guides you through the concepts you will need to understand, and she recommends the best libraries to use for robust, cross-browser development. Even if you think you know SVG and animation inside-out, you will not regret owning this essential book."

—*Chris Lilley, inventor of SVG*

"*SVG Animations* is a must-read for anyone working with SVG. Sarah Drasner has put all the most useful things she knows about animating SVG in one place, showing you how to make good design decisions around animation and how to pull it off with expert technical skill."

—*Val Head, author of* Designing Interface Animation

"Sarah Drasner is both an incredibly artistic animator and a pragmatic, detail-oriented web developer. SVG Animations provides practical solutions for animating vector graphics on the web, using the tools available today, without letting technical limitations cramp your creativity."

—*Amelia Bellamy-Royds, coauthor of* SVG Colors, Patterns & Gradients, SVG Essentials (second edition), SVG Text Layout, *and* Using SVG with CSS3 and HTML5 *(O'Reilly)*

SVG Animations
From Common UX Implementations to
Complex Responsive Animation

Sarah Drasner

Beijing · Boston · Farnham · Sebastopol · Tokyo

SVG Animations

by Sarah Drasner

Printed in the United States of America.

Published by O'Reilly Media, Inc., 1005 Gravenstein Highway North, Sebastopol, CA 95472.

O'Reilly books may be purchased for educational, business, or sales promotional use. Online editions are also available for most titles (*http://oreilly.com/safari*). For more information, contact our corporate/institutional sales department: 800-998-9938 or *corporate@oreilly.com*.

Editor: Meg Foley	**Indexer:** Wendy Catalano
Production Editor: Shiny Kalapurakkel	**Interior Designer:** David Futato
Copyeditor: Molly Ives Brower	**Cover Designer:** Karen Montgomery
Proofreader: Rachel Head	**Illustrator:** Rebecca Demarest

April 2017:   First Edition

Revision History for the First Edition

2017-03-16:   First Release

See *http://oreilly.com/catalog/errata.csp?isbn=9781491939703* for release details.

978-1-491-93970-3

[LSI]

This book is dedicated to Dizzy, my spappem.

Table of Contents

Foreword

Have you ever learned a new word, then had the opportunity to use that word in the perfect situation come up a number of times that week? That's what it feels like when you start learning SVG. To layer on the metaphors, it's like discovering your toolbox has been missing a tool all this time.

As a designer and developer, now that I've dug into SVG, I can tell you I work with it almost every single day. Not necessarily because I'm jamming SVG into projects because I can, but because it's so often the right tool for the job. After you read this book and SVG becomes your tool too, I think you too will find yourself reaching for it regularly. It will pop to mind when you're working, just like that satisfying moment when a new word you've learned comes in useful.

Perhaps you'll think of SVG when you need to replace a logo with one that will display crisply on screens of any pixel density. Perhaps you'll think of SVG when you need an icon system, a chart or graph, or a vector background pattern. Now that you're holding this book in your hands, you'll almost certainly think of SVG when you think of animation.

SVG is uniquely qualified for animation. It's the single most powerful tool there is for animation on the web. Partly that's because SVG is made of numbers. SVG essentially draws with geometry. And on the web, numbers are easy and intuitive to manipulate and animate. Perhaps you know that you can "fade out" an element—a rudimentary animation—by animating opacity from 1 to 0. So too you could animate the radius of a circle, the coordinates of a rectangle, or a point along a path.

Another reason SVG animation is so compelling is how many ways there are to do it. There are a variety of native technologies to choose from, and libraries built on top of those to help. How do you know what to choose? It requires some knowledge and consideration. Fortunately, you've made the perfect purchase.

Sarah is the ultimate tour guide for all of this. She's not just an experienced technical writer, but an accomplished vector artist and frontend developer as well. She has been bringing her own SVG art to life through animation for years and years. She knows the tools. She knows the landscape. She knows how to get to the meat of what is important about all this and explain it.

I'm not gasconading for Sarah without reason. I've worked with Sarah and ingurgitated her knowledge on SVG animation much to my benediction. If you're thinking "I'm a frontend developer already, and have gotten by just fine without this," remember that you don't reach for what you don't know. Read on, and become an SVG opsimath.

— Chris Coyier

Preface

SVG Animation: Where Art and Code Intersect

People joke that working with Scalable Vector Graphics, one must be an archaeologist, and as funny as it is, there's a lot of truth there. SVG has long lain dormant, put aside for its previous lack of support and understanding. But a few twists in the web plot have allowed for its resurgence, now-excellent support, and now-strong standing in the community:

Data visualization
> Being able to visually express concepts with the actual data is vital for communication of complex concepts.

Responsive
> In a world of thousands of devices, viewports, and pixel densities, the ability to use one graphic and have it be crisp and scale to all of them is a game-changer.

Performance
> When SVG is built properly, with reduced path points and simple shapes, it can offer tiny file sizes that bitmaps can't compete with. With properly constructed SVGs we can make our web lightning-fast and available to all.

A navigable DOM
> This point is a sleeper hit: you might not immediately notice it as a boon to development, but SVG's integration into the DOM means you have the ability to offer more information to screen readers and make your graphics truly accessible. You can also reach right inside and animate or manipulate small sections at a time. In this book, you'll discover how powerful a feature this is indeed. No crazy z-indexing and absolute positioning required!

SVG can move smoothly, freely. We've only just hit the surface of its potential. As a developer, you can feel the rush of dopamine as you watch this flexible medium bounce and snap. You can create realistic movements or stylized motions that complement your branding. The amazing thing about SVG is that you get to draw with math.

In this book, we'll cover SVG from start to finish. This means we'll look at the SVG DOM, so that working with it doesn't feel so daunting. We'll talk about designing SVGs for performance so that you have lean, clean graphics that help your site and don't hurt it. We'll talk about animating with CSS, go into some theory, and then dive deeper into some truly advanced techniques with JavaScript for beautiful and interesting effects. If you'd like to learn about designing SVGs, you'll do better with the first part of the book, while JavaScript developers will probably favor the second half. SVG brings together the worlds of design and development, so the book was written to accommodate both. I would recommend you read the first chapter, though, either way: it lays the foundation for a lot of understanding.

Animating SVGs is one of the most exciting parts of the web for me: unlocking the potential for performance, accessibility, beauty, and creativity, while avoiding some of the code ugliness and graphic hacks that responsive design sometimes entails. Working with this medium has allowed me to create amazing data visualizations that communicate clearly, tell stories, or even just make a user interaction feel a bit more refined.

Having worked for over 10 years in frontend development, learning SVG animation has helped me stave off burnout by exciting me when I fell into a rut. I hope you'll enjoy working along with the book and producing dynamic graphics for the web. It's an exciting time, and there is so much potential… only the smallest part of which has been fulfilled in web design and development to this point. I look forward to seeing the work you make with the new skills you will learn here, so that together we can push the web forward one creation at a time.

Conventions Used in This Book

The following typographical conventions are used in this book:

Italic
: Indicates new terms, URLs, email addresses, filenames, and file extensions.

`Constant width`
: Used for program listings, as well as within paragraphs to refer to program elements such as variable or function names, databases, data types, environment variables, statements, and keywords.

`Constant width bold`
: Shows commands or other text that should be typed literally by the user.

Constant width italic

Shows text that should be replaced with user-supplied values or by values determined by context.

This element signifies a tip or suggestion.

This element signifies a general note.

This element indicates a warning or caution.

Using Code Examples

We appreciate, but do not require, attribution. An attribution usually includes the title, author, publisher, and ISBN. For example: "*SVG Animations* by Sarah Drasner (O'Reilly). Copyright 2017 Sarah Drasner, 978-1-491-93970-3."

If you feel your use of code examples falls outside fair use or the permission given above, feel free to contact us at *permissions@oreilly.com*.

O'Reilly Safari

 *Safari* (formerly Safari Books Online) is a membership-based training and reference platform for enterprise, government, educators, and individuals.

Members have access to thousands of books, training videos, Learning Paths, interactive tutorials, and curated playlists from over 250 publishers, including O'Reilly Media, Harvard Business Review, Prentice Hall Professional, Addison-Wesley Professional, Microsoft Press, Sams, Que, Peachpit Press, Adobe, Focal Press, Cisco Press, John Wiley & Sons, Syngress, Morgan Kaufmann, IBM Redbooks, Packt, Adobe Press, FT Press, Apress, Manning, New Riders, McGraw-Hill, Jones & Bartlett, and Course Technology, among others.

For more information, please visit *http://oreilly.com/safari*.

How to Contact Us

Please address comments and questions concerning this book to the publisher:

O'Reilly Media, Inc.
1005 Gravenstein Highway North
Sebastopol, CA 95472
800-998-9938 (in the United States or Canada)
707-829-0515 (international or local)
707-829-0104 (fax)

We have a web page for this book, where we list errata, examples, and any additional information. You can access this page at *http://oreil.ly/2nouksg*.

To comment or ask technical questions about this book, send email to *bookquestions@oreilly.com*.

For more information about our books, courses, conferences, and news, see our website at *http://www.oreilly.com*.

Find us on Facebook: *http://facebook.com/oreilly*

Follow us on Twitter: *http://twitter.com/oreillymedia*

Watch us on YouTube: *http://www.youtube.com/oreillymedia*

Acknowledgments

I'd like to thank Meg Foley for being an incredible editor, whose guidance and thoughtfulness are always appreciated. Without her, this book would not have been possible.

I'd also like to thank the tech reviewers, Amelia Bellamy-Royds, Dudley Storey, and Val Head, whose feedback helped wrangle the book into legible shape! Thank you so much for your hard work. I'd like to thank Jack Doyle and Carl Schooff of GreenSock, Cheng Lou of React-Motion, and Oleg Solomka of mo.js too, for reviewing the content that addresses use of their libraries. Thanks also for making such amazing tools for motion on the web! I'm so grateful. Thank you Chris Lilley for inventing SVG, you're an inspiration! And thanks to Chris Coyier for the wonderful foreword as well as for being such a great mentor to me in technical writing, for CSS-Tricks and otherwise.

The biggest thanks go to Dizzy Smith, Meagan French, and Donna Ferriero for their ongoing support, especially when my ambition eyes are too big for my time-in-the-day stomach. Thank you for your care during the tough times and celebration during the milestones. You're the best!

CHAPTER 1

The Anatomy of an SVG

Scalable Vector Graphics are becoming increasingly popular as a means of serving images on the web. The format's advantages can be deduced from its name:

- SVG images are *scalable*, which in an age of increasingly varied viewport sizes is a huge boon to development. With SVG we have one graphic to rule them all that scales to all devices, and therefore can save us from subsequent HTTP requests. Even the newer CSS properties such as srcset and picture require different images to be cut for different viewports, but SVG avoids all of that extra work.
- *Vector* (rather than *raster*) means that, because they are drawn with math, SVGs tend to have greater performance and smaller file sizes.

SVG is an XML file format, and we can use it to succinctly describe shapes, lines, and text while still offering a navigable DOM; this means it can be performant *and* accessible.

In this first chapter, we'll lay the foundation for an understanding of what this DOM comprises, because we'll be reaching within it in order to create complex animations. We'll be going over some of the syntax within the SVG DOM so that you know exactly what you're manipulating and can debug as needed. We won't be doing a deep dive into everything that the SVG DOM has to offer, because it's out of the scope of this book. If you'd like more backstory, *SVG Essentials* by J. David Eisenberg and *SVG Colors, Patterns, and Gradients* by Amelia Bellamy-Royds and Kurt Cagle, both from O'Reilly, are great resources.

SVG DOM Syntax

Consider Figure 1-1, and the code that produces it:

```
<svg x="0px" y="0px" width="450px" height="100px" viewBox="0 0 450 100">
 <rect x="10" y="5" fill="white" stroke="black" width="90" height="90"/>
 <circle fill="white" stroke="black" cx="170" cy="50" r="45"/>
 <polygon fill="white" stroke="black" points="279,5 294,35 328,40 303,62
  309,94 279,79 248,94 254,62 230,39 263,35"/>
 <line fill="none" stroke="black" x1="410" y1="95" x2="440" y2="6"/>
 <line fill="none" stroke="black" x1="360" y1="6" x2="360" y2="95"/>
</svg>
```

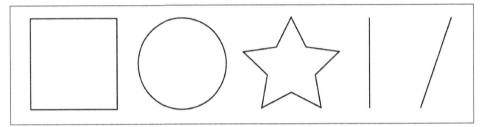

Figure 1-1. The result of the SVG code

Looking at the SVG structure, most of the markup may appear familiar to you. The syntax is easy to read because of the commonalities with HTML. In the root <svg> element, we see a declaration of x and y values—both set to 0 here, for the points in the coordinate matrix that we're starting at. The width and height are both designated, and you'll see that they correspond to the last two values in the viewBox.

viewBox and preserveAspectRatio

The SVG viewBox is a very powerful attribute, as it allows the SVG canvas to truly be infinite, while controlling and refining the viewable space. The four parameters it takes as a value are as follows: x, y, width, and height. This space is not defined in pixels, but rather is a more malleable space that can be adjusted to many different scales. Think of this as mapping out shapes and drawings on a piece of graph paper (see Figure 1-2).

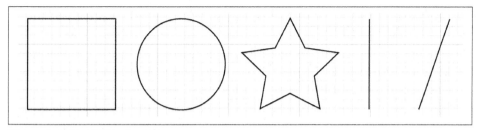

Figure 1-2. The SVG viewBox

We can define coordinates based on this system, and the system itself can be self-contained. We can then alter the size of this sheet of paper, and everything within it. If we were to designate half the width and height for the SVG, but retain the same viewBox, the result would be what is shown in Figure 1-3.

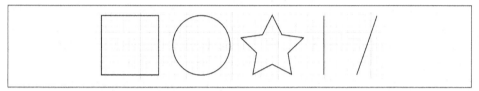

Figure 1-3. The result of the viewBox alteration

This is part of the reason why SVG is such a powerful tool for responsive development—it can adjust to multiple viewports very easily.

SVG also stores information outside the viewBox area. If we move a shape outside this space, we'll see what's shown in Figure 1-4.

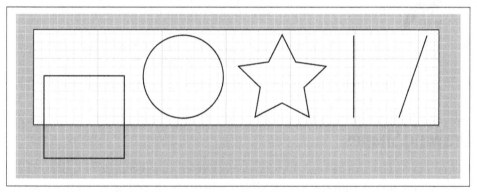

Figure 1-4. The result of moving a shape outside of the viewBox space

The white area is what the viewer sees, while the white and gray area together hold the information that the SVG actually *contains*. This feature allows the SVG to be both scalable and easy to crop on the fly. This comes in very handy in responsive applications, particularly sprites.

There is one more aspect of `viewBox` you should be aware of, invisible in this example. Most SVGs you will see on the web won't even specify it because the default, `preserveAspectRatio="xMidYMid meet`, is what most people will want more than 9 times out of 10. This forces the drawing area to adjust itself with uniform scaling.

There are several other options as well. The first parameter, `xMidYMid`, determines whether or not to uniformly scale the element, and which part of the viewport to scale from, in camel case (styled like this: camelCase). The default is to scale from the center, or `Mid`, but there are several other alignment options, such as `xMinYMax`. You may also designate `none`, in which case the aspect ratio at its default percentages will be ignored, and the element will be squashed or stretched to fill the available space.

The second parameter can be either `meet` or `slice`. `meet` will attempt to scale the graphic as much as possible to fit inside the containing `viewBox`, while keeping the aspect ratio consistent. This functionality is similar to `background-size: contain` in that the image will stay contained in the boundaries of the containing unit.

`slice` will allow the graphic within the `viewBox` to expand beyond what the user sees in the direction specified, while filling up the available area. You can think about it like `background-size: cover` in that the image will push beyond the boundaries of the containing unit to fill up the available user space.

 Further Resources

Sara Soueidan has an extremely intuitive and helpful interactive demo for you to play with in order to see this system in action (*http://bit.ly/2lNbuJv*).

Amelia Bellamy-Royds has a great resource on CSS-Tricks with tons of cool demos (*https://css-tricks.com/scale-svg/*).

Joni Trythall has a really nice resource about the `viewBox` and viewport as well (*http://bit.ly/2m8bULb*).

Drawing Shapes

Within our SVG, we've defined five shapes. `rect` refers to a rectangle or square. The x and y values, just as with the SVG itself, are where the shape begins: in this case, its upper-left corner. The shape's width and height use the same coordinate system:

```
<rect x="10" y="5" fill="white" stroke="black" width="90" height="90"/>
```

The fill and the stroke are designated here as `white` and `black`; if nothing was specified here, the fill would default to black and the stroke would be none (i.e., invisible).

circle refers to—you guessed it—a circle:

```
<circle fill="white" stroke="black" cx="170" cy="50" r="45"/>
```

cx is the point where the center of the circle lies on the x-axis, cy is the point where the center of the circle lies on the y-axis, and r is the radius. You can also use ellipse for oval shapes, the only difference being there are two radius values: rx and ry.

polygon passes an array of values in a space-separated list, defined by points:

```
<polygon fill="white" stroke="black" points="279,5 294,35 328,40 303,62 309,94
    279,79 248,94 254,62 230,39 263,35"/>
```

As you might assume, the first value refers to the *x* coordinate position, comma-separated from its matching *y* value to plot the points of this shape.

Lines are fairly straightforward:

```
<line fill="none" stroke="black" x1="410" y1="95" x2="440" y2="6"/>
```

```
<line fill="none" stroke="black" x1="360" y1="6" x2="360" y2="95"/>
```

The first point of a line is plotted at the x1 and y1 values, and the end of the line at the x2 and y2 values. I've shown two lines here so you can see that the syntax stays consistent whether the line is straight or diagonal. In terms of code, I didn't want you looking at lines sideways.

Responsive SVG, Grouping, and Drawing Paths

Now let's consider Figure 1-5 and the code that generates it:

```
<svg viewBox="0 0 218.8 87.1">
 <g fill="none" stroke="#000">
   <path d="M7.3 75L25.9 6.8s58.4-6.4 33.5 13-41.1 32.8-11.2 30.8h15.9v5.5s42.6
      18.8 0 20.6" />
   <path d="M133.1 58.2s12.7-69.2 24.4-47.5c0 0 4.1 8.6 9.5.9 0 0 5-10 10.4.9 0
      0 12.2 32.6 13.6 43 0 0 39.8 5.4 15.8 15.4-13.2 5.5-53.8
      13.1-77.4 5.9.1 0-51.9-15.4 3.7-18.6z" />
 </g>
</svg>
```

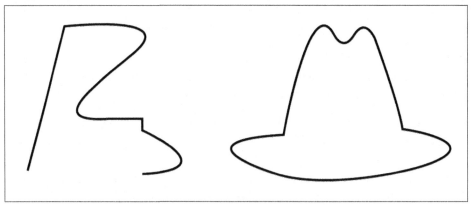

Figure 1-5. The result of removing width and height definitions

The first thing to notice about this SVG is that we've removed the width and height definitions. You can declare these elsewhere (usually in the CSS, or on the <img> or <object> element you use to embed the SVG), which makes it very malleable, especially for responsive development.

Width and Height Overrides

It's nice and easy to have CSS control all of the sizing and keep it in one place, but I sometimes leave the width and height in if I'm worried about the CSS not loading properly. If there's no fallback for the width and height inline, the SVG will scale to the available space, which can look pretty ostentatious. For that reason, you may consider writing these values inline as well. The CSS will override the presentational attributes (but not inline styles).

The SVG can now scale in percentage or viewport units, and can even be affected by media queries. The one catch is that you must declare a viewBox in this instance: it is no longer optional. The default behavior of an SVG with width and height removed and a viewBox declared is to scale to the maximum parameters of the containing element, which may be the body, a div, or just about anything else.

The second thing I'd like to point out is the <g> element. g stands for *group*, and it's a way to nest and assemble multiple elements together in the SVG DOM. You may also notice that rather than defining the fill and stroke on elements themselves, we've done so on the group, and you can see it applied across the descendants.

The last and very pertinent thing to note is the path syntax. The path begins with d, for *data*, and is always designated with the M or m (for moveTo) command as the first value. This establishes a new point. Unlike when creating a polygon/polyline, however the coordinates specified here are not always points on the final line.

Table 1-1 shows what each letter in a path means. Letters may be capital or lowercase. Capital letters specify an absolute coordinate, while lowercase establishes a relative coordinate.

Table 1-1. Path syntax

Letter	Meaning	Image, where applicable
M, m	moveTo	Start of the path
L, l	lineTo	

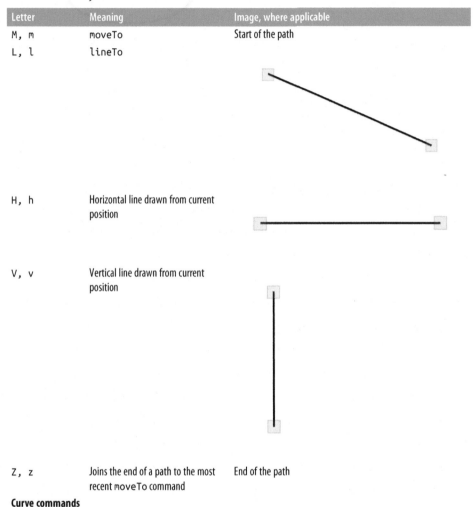

H, h	Horizontal line drawn from current position	
V, v	Vertical line drawn from current position	
Z, z	Joins the end of a path to the most recent moveTo command	End of the path

Curve commands

Letter	Meaning	Image, where applicable
C, c	Cubic Bézier	
S, s	Reflecting cubic Bézier	
Q, q	Quadratic Bézier—where both sides share the same control point	
T, t	Command control point that's been reflected	
A, a	Elliptical arc	

Revisiting Figure 1-5 and its code, you can see the difference between the paths by noting which one has a z at the end of its path data.

Delving further into path data is out of the scope of this book, but there is a great interactive demo on how path syntax works on CodePen (*http://codepen.io/ netsi1964/pen/pJzWoz*), courtesy of Sten Hougaard.

SVG on Export, Recommendations, and Optimization

You can absolutely create an SVG by hand, or create an SVG drawing with JavaScript with tools like D3 (*https://d3js.org/*). However, there are times when you may want to design and build an SVG in a graphics editor such as Adobe Illustrator (see Figure 1-6), Sketch, or Inkscape. Layers in the graphic will be exported as groups, complete with id values derived from the layer names. You may find, though, that upon export, your SVG has a lot of information that the code in the preceding examples does not:

```
<?xml version="1.0" encoding="utf-8"?>
<!-- Generator: Adobe Illustrator 18.1.1, SVG Export Plug-In . SVG Version:
    6.00 Build 0)  -->
<svg version="1.1" id="Layer_1" xmlns="http://www.w3.org/2000/svg"
    xmlns:xlink="http://www.w3.org/1999/xlink" x="0px" y="0px"
      width="218.8px" height="87.1px" viewBox="0 0 218.8 87.1"
    enable-background=
      "new 0 0 218.8 87.1" xml:space="preserve">
    <g>
      <path fill="#FFFFFF" stroke="#000000" stroke-miterlimit="10"
        d="M133.1,58.2c0,0,12.7-69.2,24.4-47.5c0,0,4.1,8.6,9.5,0.9
                c0,0,5-10,10.4,0.9c0,0,12.2,32.6,13.6,43c0,0,39.8,5.4,15.8,
        15.4c-13.2,5.5-53.8,13.1-77.4,5.9C129.5,76.8,77.5,61.4,133.1
        ,58.2z"/>
      <path fill="#FFFFFF" stroke="#000000" stroke-miterlimit="10"
      d="M6.7,61.4c0,0-3.3-55.2,20.8-54.8s-7.2,18.1,4.1,29.9
                s8.6-31.2,32.1-15.8S86.7,41,77.2,61.8C70.4,76.8,76.8,79,37.9,
      79c-0.4,0-0.9,0.1-1.3,0.1C9,81,40.1,58.7,40.1,58.7" />
    </g>
</svg>
```

Here's the earlier code again for comparison:

```
<svg viewBox="0 0 218.8 87.1">
  <g fill="none" stroke="#000">
    <path d="M7.3 75L25.9 6.8s58.4-6.4 33.5 13-41.1 32.8-11.2 30.8h15.9v5.5s42.6
        18.8 0 20.6" />
    <path d="M133.1 58.2s12.7-69.2 24.4-47.5c0 0 4.1 8.6 9.5.9 0 0 5-10 10.4.9 0
        0 12.2 32.6 13.6 43 0 0 39.8 5.4 15.8 15.4-13.2 5.5-53.8 13.1-77
        .4 5.9.1 0-51.9-15.4 3.7-18.6z" />
  </g>
</svg>
```

You can see it's much smaller: without proper optimization, you can easily bloat SVG code.

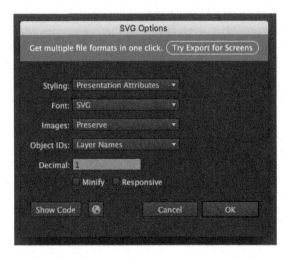
Some of this information is useful, and some we can do away with. The comment about Illustrator generating the code can certainly be removed. We also do not need the version or layer information, as the web will not use it and we're trying to transmit as few bytes as possible.

If x and y are defined as 0 (usually the case), we can strip those out, too. The only case where we'd want to leave them in is if we're working with a child SVG nested inside another SVG.

We can also strip away the XML definitions if we are using an SVG inline. I will recommend using inline SVGs for animations throughout this book because the support for animation is stronger and there are fewer gotchas. However, there are times when using an SVG as a background image works well for animation (you'll see this in

Chapters 3 and 4, when we talk about sprites). If you decide to use the SVG in an object or image, you should keep this XML markup because leaving it out can cause issues in older browsers:

```
xmlns="http://www.w3.org/2000/svg"
```

If you're not sure whether to use it or not, it's better to leave it in.

You can also optimize paths. Illustrator will export path data with unnecessary decimal places that can be removed, and may also export group markup that will clutter your code. These are only a few examples of the possibilities for compression.

Reduce Path Points

If you're going to create a hand drawing, you can trace it, but past that point you should use Object → Path → Simplify. See Figure 1-7 for a shot of the Simplify dialog box. You will need to check the Preview box, as changes made at this stage can potentially ruin the image. The image quality will tend to degrade quickly as the curve precision is lowered, so 91% is usually the lowest you can get away with. The number of points removed at this level still reduces the file size dramatically.

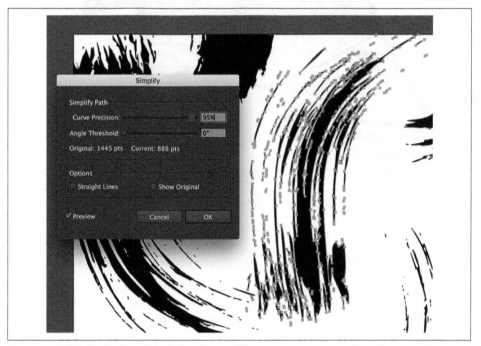

Figure 1-7. With the Simplify dialog box in Illustrator, you can reduce the size of your files dramatically

This is also probably the quickest way to accomplish this type of reduction. A more labor-intensive way that I use for smaller, unnecessarily complex pieces is to redraw them with the Pen tool. Sometimes this is very little effort for a large payoff, but it really depends on the shape.

It may seem intimidating at first, but you can use the Pen tool to quickly make more complex areas, using the Pathfinder tool to merge them all together (see Figure 1-8). If it doesn't look quite right, don't fear! You can reduce the opacity a little (so that you can see what you're trying to emulate in the shape underneath), then use the Direct Selection tool, (A in quick keys, or the white arrow on the toolbar) to drag the points of the shape around until you get a more refined result. It also never hurts to zoom in a bit to see fine details.

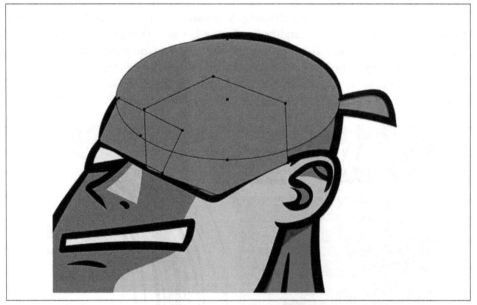

Figure 1-8. Draw shapes quickly and merge them together to create complex paths without a lot of path points

Optimization Tools

You don't need to strip this information out by hand, though. There are many great tools for optimizing SVGs and they offer more ways to help trim your code, such as rounding and rewriting numbers, merging path data, removing unneeded groups, and more.

The following list includes some of the available open source tools. The ones that visually show the output tend to be the most useful, as you can see how optimization may change the result:

SVGOMG (https://jakearchibald.github.io/svgomg/)
Jake Archibald has created a really nice web-based GUI for the terminal-based SVGO (see below). This tool is the most robust and easy to work with, and includes many toggle optimization options. SVGOMG shows the relative visual output and the byte-saving comparison after optimization.

SVG Editor (http://petercollingridge.appspot.com/svg-editor-)
Peter Collingridge's SVG Editor is very similar to SVGOMG, with slightly fewer options. A nice feature is that you can edit the SVG right in another panel in case you need to adjust the output just slightly. It's web-based, with a nice visual interface.

SVGO (https://github.com/svg/svgo-)
SVGO is terminal-based, with no visual GUI; however, you can add one with SVGO-GUI (*https://github.com/svg/svgo-gui*). This requires a bit more setup but is a workflow boon if you're more comfortable working in your terminal than popping in and out of the browser. The functionality powers SVGOMG as well.

Please be aware that you will need to change and adjust optimization settings depending on what you're trying to achieve in your animation. Get comfortable with adjusting these options rather than settling for the defaults, as doing so will save you considerable time later. You may find that a very busy animation requires repeated optimizations while you're developing; for this reason, I recommend leaving your graphics editor and optimization tool open while working with your code editor to make your workflow as seamless as possible.

Default Export Settings to Be Aware Of

Be mindful of some of the defaults when you're exporting. The ones that I find myself checking and unchecking the most are:

- *Clean IDs*—This will remove any carefully named layers you may have.
- *Collapse useless groups*—You might have grouped them to animate them all together, or just to keep things organized.
- *Merge paths*—Nine times out of 10 this one is OK, but sometimes merging a lot of paths keeps you from being able to move elements in the DOM around independently.
- *Prettify*—This is only necessary when you need to continue working with the SVG code in an editor.

CHAPTER 2

Animating with CSS

You may find working with SVG code feels very familiar, mostly because an SVG has a DOM, just like standard HTML markup. This is hugely valuable when working with CSS animations, as manipulating markup with CSS is already a very comfortable process for most frontend developers.

For a very brief review, let's first establish that a CSS animation is created by defining two parameters. First, there are the keyframes themselves:

```
@keyframes animation-name-you-pick {
  0% {
    background: blue;
    transform: translateX(0);
  }
  50% {
    background: purple;
    transform: translateX(50px);
  }
  100% {
    background: red;
    transform: translateX(100px);
  }
}
```

Keyframe Syntax Hint

You can also define from and to instead of percentages. If you declare nothing in either the initial keyframe or the ending keyframe, the animation will use the default or declared properties on the element. It may be worth double-checking your work in all browsers if you do remove them, though, due to strange and inconsistent browser bugs.

After you define the keyframe values, you have two options for animation syntax declaration. Here's an example of the long form, with each declaration defined separately:

```
.ball {
  animation-name: animation-name-you-pick;
  animation-duration: 2s;
  animation-delay: 2s;
  animation-iteration-count: 3;
  animation-direction: alternate;
  animation-timing-function: ease-in-out;
  animation-fill-mode: forwards;
}
```

And here's the shorthand (my preferred method, as it uses less code):

```
.ball {
  animation: animation-name-you-pick 2s 2s 3 alternate ease-in-out forwards;
}
```

The order of the declarations is interchangeable in a space-separated list, except for the number values, which must be defined in this order: duration, delay, and iteration count.

Let's apply this animation to this very simple .ball div (shown in Figure 2-1):

```
.ball {
  border-radius: 50%;
  width: 50px;
  height: 50px;
  margin: 20px; // so that it's not hitting the edge of the page
  background: black;
}
```

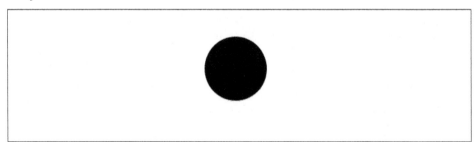

Figure 2-1. The result of applying .ball div

We get the result in Figure 2-2, with interstitial states shown less opaque.

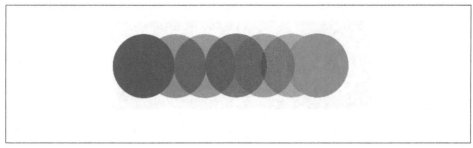

Figure 2-2. The result of adjusting the ball div

You can see all the code in action in a demo I created (*http://bit.ly/2lSB8KZ*).

For more information and further detail about each animation property, such as what animation-fill-mode is, what eases are available in CSS, and which properties are animatable, see *Transitions and Animations in CSS* by Estelle Weyl (O'Reilly).

You can also consult *Pro CSS3 Animation*, by Dudley Storey (Apress).

Animating with SVG

Let's say instead of drawing the ball with CSS, we had drawn it with SVG. We know how to do that from the last chapter. To get the same black circle as in Figure 2-1, we would write:

```
<svg width="70px" height="70px" viewBox="0 0 70 70">
  <circle fill="black" cx="45" cy="45" r="25"/>
</svg>
```

We define the radius as half of 50, so 25 px. Then we move the center of the circle on both the x- and y-axes (cx and cy) to half the radius, plus that 20 px margin we added in the CSS. We could also use margin on the SVG element to move it, but here I'm illustrating that you can draw coordinates directly in the SVG itself. If we move the circle over, though, the viewBox has to be larger to accommodate these coordinates: it's the width plus the margin of space to the edge.

Now, if we place a class on the whole SVG called ball, using the same animation declaration, we get what's shown in Figure 2-3.

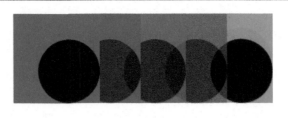

Figure 2-3. The result of placing the ball class on the SVG

What happened here? It still moved across, as we were expecting. But the background is filling in the full background of the SVG, thus the entire viewBox. That's not really what we want. So what happens if we move that class and target the circle instead? See Figure 2-4.

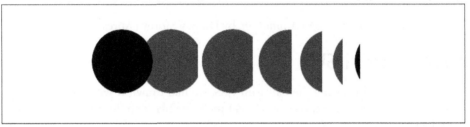

Figure 2-4. The result of moving the ball class

You may have guessed why we have this output. There are two reasons:

1. The circle is moving inside the viewBox. Remember, if we move an internal SVG attribute, the viewBox will quite literally be a window through which we view these elements. So if we move the circle without making the viewBox large enough to accommodate those coordinates, it will be cut off when the circle moves out of the viewBox.

2. The SVG DOM looks like the HTML DOM, but it's slightly different. We don't use background on SVG attributes; we use fill and stroke. An external stylesheet will also have a hard time overriding what is defined inline within the SVG. So let's take out the fill definition, and move that into our stylesheet.

The resulting code should be this:

```
<svg width="200px" height="70px" viewBox="0 0 200 70">
<circle class="ball3" cx="45" cy="45" r="25"/>
</svg>
```

And here's the CSS:

```
.ball3 {
  animation: second-animation 2s 2s 3 alternate ease-in-out forwards;
}

@keyframes second-animation {
  0% {
    fill: blue;
    transform: translateX(0);
  }
  50% {
    fill: purple;
    transform: translateX(50px);
  }
  100% {
    fill: red;
    transform: translateX(100px);
  }
}
```

The result is Figure 2-5, but with an SVG instead of an HTML div.

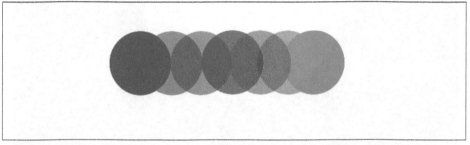

Figure 2-5. The result of taking out the fill definition and moving it to the stylesheet

Benefits of Drawing with SVG

So, why learn SVG when you could build something in CSS-styled HTML and animate that way?

First of all, even that small, simple circle was four lines less than the CSS version. SVG was built for drawing—unlike CSS, which was built for presentational formatting. Let's look at the code for the star from the first chapter of this book:

```
<polygon fill="white" stroke="black" points="279,5 294,35 328,40
   303,62 309,94 279,79 248,94 254,62 230,39 263,35 "/>
```

It would be incredibly difficult to draw a star in CSS with such a small amount of code, and impossible for the code to be that concise once compiled, if using a preprocessor.

Figure 2-6 is something I drew in Illustrator.

Figure 2-6. An example of the ease of Illustrator

We could also probably draw this in CSS, but to what end? If you're working with a designer on a project, having them draw something for you in CSS is not typically an option, and drawings that you want to animate can get much more complex than this. In SVG you can also make the whole image scale easily, and therefore, your whole animation can be responsive.

All of the information for the illustration is just *2 KB gzipped*, and it can fill up a whole screen. That's pretty amazing if you consider raster image alternatives.

Applying what we just learned about the circle, we can look at some of these shapes and think about what we can do with them. We could group all of the parts of the cow together and make it jump over the moon. We could make the astronaut's "surprised" expression disappear and appear. We can even make the helmet go up and down so it looks like the astronaut is looking up. (That is actually what I did in the final animation.)

Silky-Smooth Animation

It's tempting to use all of the same properties that you use to affect layout with CSS: `margin`, `top`, `left`, etc. But browsers do not update values for all properties equally. To animate cheaply, your best bet is to use *transforms* and *opacity*. That might seem limiting, but transforms offer translation (positioning), scale, and rotation. Using these in combination with opacity can be extremely powerful. It's surprising how much can be achieved with these properties in standard animations.

Throughout this book, I will use these properties wherever possible while demonstrating various techniques. It is important to note that SVG DOM elements are currently hardware-accelerated only in some browsers (for instance, hardware acceleration is supported in Firefox but not Chrome), but you should still be moving the SVG DOM with transforms, not margins or other CSS positioning.

At the time of publishing, Microsoft Internet Explorer (IE) and Edge did not support transforms on SVG elements at all—but you can vote on these issues and more on the Windows Developer Feedback site (*http://bit.ly/2lkk4f8*).

Until this is supported, your best bet for Edge is using either native SVG transforms (which are a pain and you'll need JavaScript for) or the GreenSock Animation API, which has support back to IE9.

For more information on how to properly keep your layout repaint costs low (these are Chrome-specific resources), check out Jank Free (*http://jankfree.org/*) and High Performance Animations (*http://bit.ly/2lPFlRo*).

For information on the costs of individual properties, see CSS Triggers (*http://csstriggers.com/*).

CHAPTER 3

CSS Animation and Hand-Drawn SVG Sprites

SVG performs extremely well as an icon format, but we'll move a step further and use SVG sprites in performant complex animations using three different techniques. The first two are closely related to cel animation, while the third, detailed in Chapter 4, is a technique I recommend for more complex responsive animations and interactive SVGs.

From a design perspective, this is a more advanced animation technique. We're discussing it at this point in the book because the actual animation can be created purely with CSS. The book follows a progression based on animation technology (first CSS, then JavaScript libraries, then bare-metal JS), but feel free to skip around; Chapter 7 offers a comparison of animation techniques.

Keyframe Animation with steps() and SVG Sprites, Two Ways

If you've ever seen a *Looney Tunes* or old Disney animation, you might have been impressed with the fluid movement, considering that every frame was hand-drawn. Such effects are possible on the web with SVG sprites, and we can stand on the shoulders of previous animators while employing new development techniques.

Of all web-based animation techniques, step animation most closely resembles these old hand-drawn cel animations. *Cel* is short for "celluloid," a type of transparent material used by animators to draw on top of their previous drawings, thereby defining a sequence and creating the illusion of movement. This technique functioned a bit like a flip book. Each drawing was captured on film, frame by frame. There were usually several layers to these drawings to save time—you wouldn't want to redraw the background again and again just to show the same scene.

In order to save steps in drawing, the background would be painted, and then the character or sometimes even just pieces of the character's face, like the mouth or eyes —would be adjusted. See Figures 3-1 and 3-2 for an example of the layering.

Figure 3-1. Hand-painted cel with transparency (image courtesy of John Gunn)

Cel Animations as Scoping

You can think of this technique like writing web page templates: you start from the base template and create smaller pieces, so you can manage an individual thing that's happening in one piece separately from everything else.

Figure 3-2. Hand-painted cel with painted background behind (image courtesy of John Gunn)

We can mimic this analog process by using a single motionless background, then quickly showing a series of images on top. This gives the illusion of movement without any real interpolation. Instead of a series of separate image files, we will simultaneously reduce the number of HTTP requests and simplify our keyframes by using a single SVG sprite sheet (Figure 3-3). This technique is great for more complex shapes and expressive movement than simple transforms can offer.

Because this technique relies heavily on design, we'll go through the design workflow first, and then go through the code. You can find what the final animation looks like on my CodePen page (*http://codepen.io/sdras/pen/LEzdea/*).

Typically when showing interpolated (i.e., rapidly changing) images on the web, we should push the maximum frames per second (fps) possible to achieve the silkiest animation. This technique is one exception to that rule. Since we have to draw every single frame, we're going to try to get as much bang for our hand-drawn buck as possible (see Figure 3-4). Years ago, animators spent a lot of time trying to find a good balance between realistic movement and the fewest number of drawings. Old film was shot at 24 fps, and animators largely regarded "shooting on twos" (meaning one drawing over two frames, or 12 fps) as the standard for an illusion of movement. Drop to anything lower than this, and your eye will discern a slight choppiness (which some animators even used as a creative decision!). We'll use their work in finding these bounds of illusion to our benefit, stick to the 12 fps rule, and create a 21-part drawing for a 1.8 s animation. The 21 here comes from the number of frames that we chose, but can be any number you like.

Figure 3-3. Stills for our splash animation

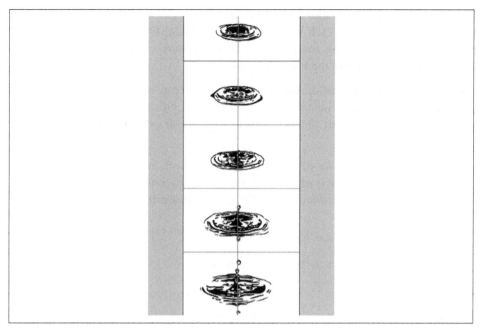

Figure 3-4. Our artboard with guides and frame-by-frame drawing

The "Drawing in Illustrator with a Template" Way

There are two ways of creating the series of drawings for this type of animation; both work equally well, but they use different automation processes for the images. The challenge we face in each workflow is keeping the drawing steadily placed in the center of the frame throughout a large sprite; even the best drawing will look flawed if the drawing jumps as we run through each frame.

I use Illustrator for this technique, but you could theoretically use Sketch or any other graphics editor. First, we decide how big the animation is and multiply that number by 21 in one direction (the number of frames in our animation), determining the length of our artboard. We drag a box around that area and choose Object → Path → Split Into Grid. Then we enter the number of rows we want (or columns, if we wish to make a horizontal sprite sheet) and click OK. Finally, we choose View → Guides → Make Guides, and our template is all set.

If you're drawing directly in the graphics editor, I recommend placing your first drawing within the first box, and creating a box around it that frames it within the guides. You can then copy everything into the next box (including the box frame) using the alignment line or Shift + drag, which will keep it steady. Use the box frame again to fit it into the next guide's space.

Using the Direct Selection tool (the white arrow), you can then drag and reshape the pieces of your image for each frame. Fair warning: don't be tempted to front-load your work here by copying and pasting it all at the start—this process works best if you build each frame from the previous one.

You can also do a screencast of something so that you can walk through the stills and place each image in the Illustrator doc and trace it, either with Illustrator's native trace functionality, or with the Pen tool for a hand-drawn feel and more concise paths.

At the end of this process we will have a long sprite sheet. We can export that directly as an SVG as well as a PNG, which we'll use as a fallback with a body class hook in Modernizr (for more about Modernizr, see "Using Modernizr" on page 30):

```
.splash {
  background: url('splash-sprite2.svg');
  ...
  animation: splashit 1.8s steps(21) infinite;
}

/* fallback */
.no-svg .splash {
  background: url('splash-sprite2.png');
}
```

At this point, though, fallbacks might not be necessary, so it's recommended you check your analytics and consult the *caniuse.com* tables for SVG support.

The "Drawing in an SVG Editor or on Paper Frame-by-Frame and Using Grunticon to Sprite" Way

The first process will still look like an Illustrator drawing, but you may want a hand-drawn feel. If this is the case, it's very easy to draw by hand and scan it in. Old animation studios used lightboxes and celluloid sheets so that they could trace their previous drawing incrementally. You don't necessarily need these materials to try this technique, though. By placing a lamp underneath a glass table, you can easily make a poor man's lightbox. This setup shines enough light so that you can see through even regular opaque copy paper. To create each new frame, place a piece of paper or vellum over your last drawing and change the drawing slightly until you have a series. You can then scan this set of drawings and vectorize them, placing them correctly with reduced opacity and guides.

If you'd rather draw each piece frame by frame in the editor but don't know how many frames you will be creating, you can draw each one separately, shifting the image slightly each time and saving every new version to a folder. Illustrator's new export settings are good enough that that you can do so without all the old cruft and comments. Be sure to export with Export → SVG rather than Save As → SVG. You must make sure that what you're initially saving is indeed an SVG and not an AI (or any other) file type. You can then use Grunticon (*http://www.grunticon.com*) to compress and sprite them automatically. There's a great article on CSS-Tricks (*http://css-tricks.com/inline-svg-grunticon-fallback/*) explaining how to do so. Notably, Grunticon also generates a fallback PNG automatically.

Personally, I think if you draw each frame by hand, it makes the most sense to just make sure the placement on each artboard is consistent and use Grunticon, but the Illustrator template technique has the benefit of allowing you to see all of your work at once, which gives you more of a holistic understanding of what you're making.

Simple Code for Complex Movement

This type of sprite makes use of the smallest amount of code for the most amount of believable movement. We intentionally keep the code DRY (an acronym that means *don't repeat yourself*), simple, and clean. The greatest thing about this type of movement is that we rely enough on the sprite to not need a lot of code to achieve an illusion of movement through space.

We absolutely position a smaller area of movement because we want to show a consistent experience across desktop and mobile. Our aim is to cycle through the entire image, but stop momentarily at each individual picture in the image, and thankfully, steps() in CSS allows us to do just that. We've already done a lot of the heavy lifting in our design, so the code to create the effect is very small.

There's no need for complex percentages and keyframes. All we need to do is use the image height as a negative integer on the 100% keyframe value for the background position:

```
@keyframes splashit {
  100% { background-position: 0 -3046px; }
}
```

Here, we don't have to use .container-fluid, because it's easy to have the SVG take up the whole screen on mobile devices. In the splash div, we animate using steps() for the number of frames we had in the SVG:

```
.splash {
  background: url('splash-sprite2.svg');
  ...
  animation: splashit 1.8s steps(21) infinite;
}
```

Using an SVG rather than a PNG gives us the advantage of a crisp image on all displays, but it's easy to provide a fallback. We use Modernizr to create a class hook on body and can still animate it with the PNG we created:

```
/* fallback */
.no-svg .splash {
  background: url('splash-sprite2.png');
}
```

We don't simply use the PNG because at different resolutions it will look fuzzy, while the SVG will remain crisp.

Using Modernizr

Modernizr (*https://modernizr.com/*) is a feature detection library. It allows you to work with advanced features on the web while providing fallbacks, or progressively enhance features by checking to see if they are available. It's a highly customizable library that provides classes on the body element that you can hook into for different experiences, like the .no-svg tag in the preceding example. I highly suggest working with a custom build for your unique purposes—the entire library is a lot of overhead, and you'll likely only use a small portion of it.

Simple Walk Cycle

If you take the steps() value out of the last animation, you'll see something interesting. Instead of creating a seamless moving drawing, the background rolls through. We can use that to our advantage for a nice layered background with spatial placement and movement.

Let's consider a walk cycle (*http://codepen.io/sdras/pen/azEBEZ*), that shows a ghostly figure walking through a looping, multidimensional, outlined landscape.

We can create this using the previous technique with the cels/steps, with drawings that show a walk cycle. We'll use a manual animation technique to change the color by shifting the color in each frame. Alternatively, we could have used a filter with a shift for hue-rotate, but as long as we are creating all of these frames by hand the amount of work required to change the color here is minimal, and the cost of the filters on performance, while not huge, is one we can do without.

CSS Filter Demos

If you do choose to work with filters, there are a number of sites that demo great capabilities with CSS filter effects. Here are just a few:

- HTML5 Demos (*http://bit.ly/2lSARYv*), the source of the preceding images
- CSS Filter Playground by Bennett Feely (*http://bennettfeely.com/filters/*)
- CSSReflex (*http://www.cssreflex.com/css-generators/filter/*)
- My personal favorite, CSSGram (*http://una.im/CSSgram/*) by Una Kravets, which mixes filters to make some great Instagram-like effects

Keep in mind that animating filters can be very costly. I tend to avoid animating them, or use a `setTimeout` that will apply the attribute or CSS strictly for the time I need it, and then remove it.

It's still important that the `steps()` and `animation-duration` ratio fall around the 12 fps range. We can scroll through each version of the images presented by animating the background position of the SVG sprite sheet. In order to keep everything consistent, we've made all of the background images the same size (see Figure 3-5), which lends itself well to the use of an `@extend` if you're working with Sass:

```
/*--extend--*/
.area {
  width: 600px;
  height: 348px;
}

.fore, .mid, .bk, .container { @extend .area; }
```

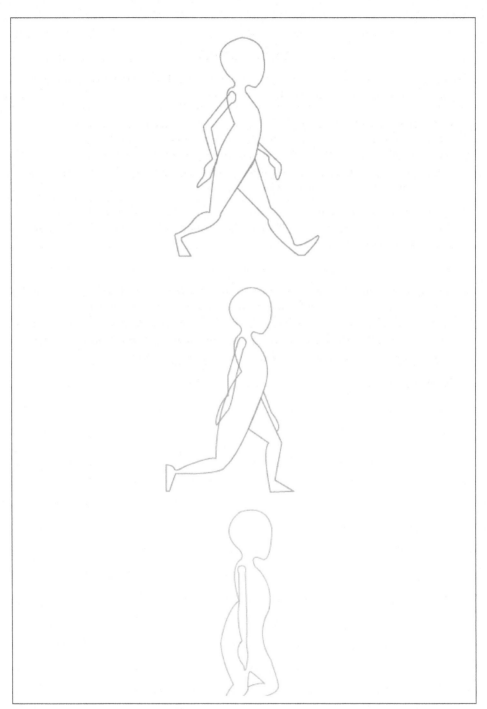

Figure 3-5. Fluidity and consistency in images

To create the impression of fluid linear infinite movement, the three background images must be able to repeat seamlessly on the x-axis so that when they scroll through there are no seams. This can be achieved by making each end identical, or, as in this case, using an image that is sparse enough that it can completely flow through (Figure 3-6). If you're working with the latter, it's important to marry the beginning state and end state in a graphics editor like Illustrator or Sketch to ensure it looks OK while you're building the graphic.

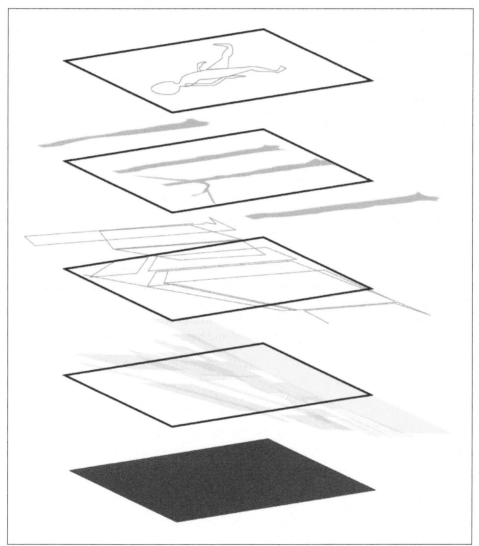

Figure 3-6. We'll layer SVGs to create an illusion of depth

Each element uses the same keyframe values, but we set apart their animations with an incremental decrease in seconds the further back their z-index goes. If you look around you, things that are closer to you are in sharper contrast and appear to move faster than things that are further away. Our animation will mimic this effect by increasing the second integer (and thus having longer animations) for the SVGs in the background. This yields a nice *parallax* effect. There are three parallaxed background images in this example that don't include the figure:

```
.fore {
  background: url('fore.svg');
  animation: bk 7s -5s linear infinite;
}

.mid {
  background: url('mid.svg');
  animation: bk 15s -5s linear infinite;
}

.bk {
  background: url('bkwalk2.svg');
  animation: bk 20s -5s linear infinite;
}

@keyframes bk {
  100% { background-position: 200% 0; }
}
```

We don't need multiple intervals for this kind of animation, because keyframes will interpolate values for us. In the event that the number of pixels in the scrolling sprite sheets changes in the future, we don't have to update the amounts, because we set it with a percentage. The use of negative delays ensures that the animation is running from the start. All of the SVGs are optimized and have a PNG fallback.

CHAPTER 4

Creating a Responsive SVG Sprite

The "scalable" part of SVG is perhaps the most powerful aspect of the graphics format. Using the `viewBox` attribute and our knowledge of shapes and paths, we can crop an SVG to any size on the fly, knowing that our intentions within the coordinate space will be preserved.

If we remove the `width` and `height` attributes from a common SVG, we'll see something interesting. The SVG expands itself to the full width of the viewport, maintaining the aspect ratio of everything within the DOM.

If we use CSS keyframes or JavaScript to move SVG elements such as `circle` or `path` while scaling this SVG up or down, the increments that they will move will scale as well, along with the graphic. *This means that if you scale a complex SVG using percentages, a flexbox, or other techniques, your animation will scale accordingly.* You don't have to adjust anything for mobile or other sizes; you can focus on writing the code correctly one time.

The completed animation is completely scalable. In the following CodePen example (*http://codepen.io/sdras/full/jPLgQM/*), you can randomly resize the animation while it's running and watch it instantly adjust. This is very useful for responsive development. The animation in Figure 4-1 uses a completely fluid approach.

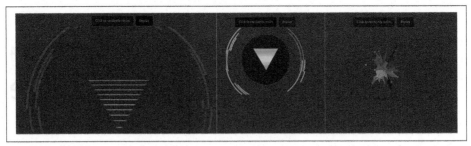

Figure 4-1. Different states of the same animation at different sizes

We design the whole thing first, and then slowly reveal things. Figure 4-2 is what our initial SVG (before we add any animation) looks like.

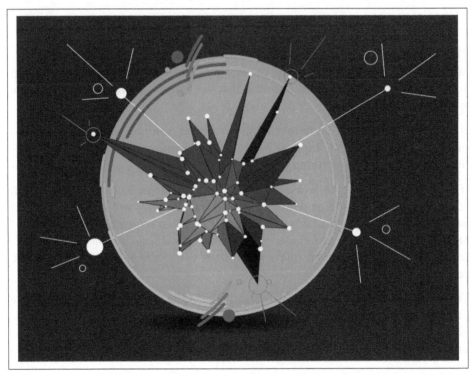

Figure 4-2. Original design in Illustrator—we design everything first, and then slowly reveal things

We could also design for responsiveness SVG in two other ways. In this chapter, we'll do a deep dive into a technique that uses SVG sprites, similar to the ones we created in Chapter 3. This is easy to work with in CSS. In Chapter 15, we'll cover a more advanced JavaScript approach as we hide, show, collapse, and rearrange our content.

SVG Sprites and CSS for Responsive Development

Joe Harrison has demonstrated a really nice way of collapsing SVG sprites for less visual information on mobile (*http://responsiveicons.co.uk/*), shown in Figure 4-3. We're
going to use that to our advantage and create a similar, incrementally more complex
sprite as we shift viewports from mobile to desktop.

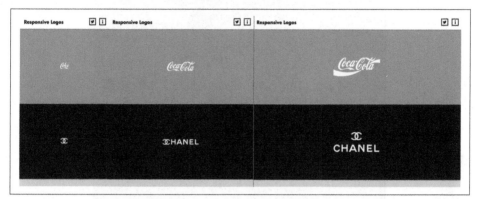

Figure 4-3. Joe Harrison's very impressive SVG logo sprites

As our screen sizes shrink and grow, the graphic follows suit and condenses or reveals
visual complexity. It's helpful to the user to not be served visually complex graphics
on small displays, where too much information can become noise. Animations can be
modified with the same considerations as the typography and layout, adjusting to the
viewport and clarifying the design.

We're going to be working with a responsive illuminated drop-capital letter (*http://
codepen.io/sdras/full/xbyopy/*) to show how a standalone illustration can adjust
(Figure 4-4). The design was inspired by the *Book of Kells*, an incredibly decorated
medieval manuscript, to show how a standalone drawing can adjust to different viewport sizes. We start from this design, which we'll use as our "map." Other people plan
differently, working in-browser or making sketches; choose whatever method makes
you most productive.

Figure 4-4. Designing our "map"

Grouping and DRYing It Out

Now that we know how the final product appears, we can refactor the design to group like sections together, based on what's most important for the associated viewport width. We can also simplify the design by identifying shapes used in both the first and second versions, keeping just one copy of each shared shape.

All of the elements are assigned semantic ID names such as "mountain" or "bridge." The most detailed shapes also get a shared ID that we can progressively show for larger viewports. If the first illustration is kells1, the group particular to the second illustration is kells2, and the last is kells3.

In order to make the SVG scalable to shared container values, the last illustration becomes the same size as the first; SVG's built-in responsiveness will take care of the rest.

We end up creating only two areas of the sprite sheet, with both having the same width so that we can scale the whole image at once (Figure 4-5). The top graphic is more complex; it holds information for both the tablet and desktop instances.

Figure 4-5. The sprite once we reduce repetition and get it ready for export

Once we have this view, we run it through SVGOMG, using the web-based GUI to check that there's no distortion and toggling off the option to Clean IDs and also Collapse Useless Groups. We can later change the IDs to classes if we wish and clean up some of the cruft from the export. I do this by hand or with find and replace, but there are myriad ways to accomplish it.

The optimized SVG is placed inline in the HTML rather than included as a source URL background image like in the previous techniques. Now we can set areas to hide and show with a mobile-first implementation:

```
@media screen and ( min-width: 701px ) {
  .kells3, .kells2 {
    display: none;
  }
}
```

We can also adjust the animation parameters slightly, depending on the viewport, in order to refine the movement for each version:

```
[class^="mountain"], [class^="grass"] {
  ...
  transform: skew(1.5deg);
}

@media screen and ( min-width: 500px ) {
  [class^="mountain"], [class^="grass"] {
    transform: skew(2deg);
  }
}
```

At this point the width and height are removed from the SVG and we can add in `preserveAspectRatio="xMidYMid meet"` (though that's the default, so it's not strictly necessary) to make the SVG fluid. With these alterations, it will adjust to the container size instead, which we set based on percentages (a. flexbox or any other responsive container would work here too):

```
.initial {
  width: 50%;
  float: left;
  margin: 0 7% 0 0;
}
```

The viewBox Trick

There is one catch—even if we assign the bottom layer a class and hide it, there will be an empty gap where the `viewBox` still accounts for that space. In order to account for that area, we can change the `viewBox` in the SVG to show only the top portion:

```
viewBox="0 0 490 474"
```

That will work, but only for the two larger versions. The smallest version is now obscured, as the `viewBox` is providing a window into another portion of the SVG sprite sheet, so we will need to adjust it. This is akin to changing the background position in CSS to show different areas of a sprite sheet. But because we're adjusting an SVG attribute, we will need JavaScript, as CSS doesn't yet have that capability:

```
var shape = document.getElementById("svg");

// media query event handler
if (matchMedia) {
        var mq = window.matchMedia("(min-width: 500px)");
        mq.addListener(WidthChange);
        WidthChange(mq);
}
// media query change
function WidthChange(mq) {
  if (mq.matches) {
    shape.setAttribute("viewBox", "0 0 490 474");
  } else {
    shape.setAttribute("viewBox", "0 490 500 500");
  }
};
```

 There's an ongoing discussion of adding these types of adjustments into the CSS spec on the W3C's GitHub page (*https://github.com/w3c/fxtf-drafts/issues/7*); Jake Archibald has also raised the issue (*http://bit.ly/2mANBmP*). If the proposal is adopted, you will be able to update all of the `viewBox` changes in media queries and keep presentation implementation in one language.

Now when we scroll the browser window horizontally the viewport will shift to display only the part of the SVG we want to expose. Our code is now primed and ready to animate.

Responsive Animation

When we export from a graphics editor, we have a unique ID for every different element. My preference for repeated elements is to use classes, so I did a find and replace of IDs to classes (Illustrator will still add some unique numbers to the names of each class, but we can target them using a CSS `attributeStartsWith` selector):

```
[class^="mountain"], [class^="grass"] {
  animation: slant 9s ease-in-out infinite both;
  transform: skew(2deg);
}
```

You'll see here that we begin with a transform set on that element; this keeps the keyframe animation nice and concise. The animation will assume that the 0% keyframe corresponds to the initial state of the element; to create a very efficient loop, we can define only the changes halfway through the animation sequence:

```
@keyframes slant {
  50% { transform: skew(-2deg); } }
}
```

Some elements, such as the dots and stars, share a common animation, so we can reuse the declaration, adjusting the timing and delay as needed. We use a negative offset for the delay because we want it to appear as though it's running from the start, even though the element animations are staggered. Animation keyframes will use the default positioning set on the element as the 0% and 100% keyframes unless they are specified otherwise. We use this to our benefit to write the least code possible:

```
@keyframes blink {
  50% { opacity: 0; }
}

[class^="star"] {
  animation: blink 2s ease-in-out infinite both;
}

[class^="dot"] {
  animation: blink 5s -3s ease-in-out infinite both;
}
```

We also need to add a viewport <meta> tag, which gives us control over the page's width and scaling on different devices. The most common one will do:

```
<meta name="viewport" content="width=device-width, initial-scale=1">
```

CHAPTER 5

UI/UX Animations with No External Libraries

In the previous chapters we've mostly covered standalone SVG animations. In this chapter, we'll go over more common use cases of UI and UX elements that can be implemented with SVG and animated with CSS. In particular, we'll work through a common UX pattern of a transforming icon, which will allow you to see how something is built from start to finish, integrating the workflow into your own development process.

Animation gets a bad rap sometimes, often because we don't consider its power. When users are scanning a website (or any environment, or photo), they are attempting to build a spatial map. During this process, nothing quite commands attention like something in motion.

We are biologically trained to notice motion: evolutionarily speaking, our survival depends on it. For this reason, animation, when done well, can guide your users. It can aid and reinforce these spatial maps, and give us a sense that we understand the UX more deeply: we retrieve information and put it back where it came from instead of something popping into and out of place.

Context-Shifting in UX Patterns

Before we get into *how* to build typical UI/UX interactions into SVG animations, let's go over the *why*. It's important to get the technique down, but it's just as important to use animation correctly.

Have you ever had a day at work where people kept interrupting you and putting you to different types of tasks? Work feels more frustrating when you can't get into a flow-based working style, and it makes you feel more disorganized and unproductive. It follows that using a website works the same way.

When you visit a website, your brain uses *saccades*—a series of rapid eye movements —to create spatial relationships. You never really "look" at an image: your eye moves constantly to understand where things are placed in the picture, creating a mental map of the image. See Figure 5-1 for an example of a saccade heatmap.

Figure 5-1. A heatmap of all eye movement across a website during saccade to create spatial awareness

When we create a website, we're creating a mental map for our users. Changes we make to site interactions can break that mental map. Modals are a good example: they often pop up out of nowhere, shattering the user's experience, and are an example of what I call "brute-force UX."

An animation that reduces friction in context-shifting succeeds by honoring the user's mental map: the user will retrieve and access things from consistent areas, the UX flows with user's needs, and the whole experience feels more fluid. Creating animations that help guide your users takes a bit of thinking, so let's break down some ways we can do it:

- Morphing
- Revealing
- Isolation
- Style
- Anticipatory cues
- Interaction
- Space conservation

Before we dive into solutions, it's important to note that any one of these can be *overdone*. Again, our brains have evolved to take particular note of something in motion. This evolutionary trait is in place to keep us safe and alert; the part of your brain that kicks up adrenaline is also triggered when something unexpected moves on the screen. The web is a static, dull site without animation; but when it comes to UX animation, subtlety is key.

To show how an animation can retain context for a user, I've built an example (*http:// codepen.io/sdras/full/qOdwdB/*) that we'll be referring back to repeatedly as we cover these premises (see Figure 5-2).

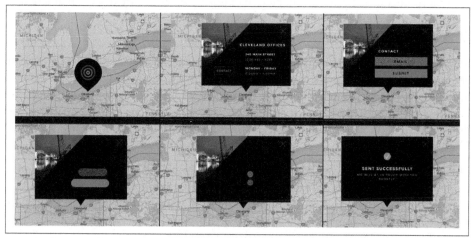

Figure 5-2. All of these states come from and return to one element

Morphing

Morphing is probably the simplest way to help users retain context. Morphing means that the same element can become multiple pieces of information in different contexts, guiding the user's flow without changing anything very abruptly. Consider the animation in Figure 5-2. There are many forms of morphing in the one interactive element used in the CodePen example. In this example, one frame morphs into the next: the pin expands to create the dialog, the contact button becomes the title, the text boxes shrink to become the loader dots, and so on, to provide a smooth user experience.

Both SVG and CSS are good options for these kinds of UI animations. I've found from working with both that each has its strengths and weaknesses. CSS easily interpolates round to square and back again with border-radius (*http://bit.ly/2lHGrjB*). It can also handle large quantities of scale transforms gracefully; SVG, beyond a few great numbers, will appear pixelated before recovering. However, SVG is built for drawing. It is well suited for complex shapes.

You can tween path or even shape data with JavaScript and GreenSock's MorphSVG plug-in (*https://greensock.com/morphSVG*). This is an unbeatable tool for this kind of technique: unlike Snap.svg or even the poorly supported SMIL, MorphSVG allows you to easily transform between *uneven amounts* of path data, which allows for tons of wonderful effects. If you're interested in learning more about what you can do with SVG morphing, please refer to Chapter 10 of this book, where we discuss it at length.

Revealing

Revealing is a very simple method of retaining context for the user, but revealing can be done in a way that breaks the user's context as well. Take your typical modal, for instance. This is an example of UX that comes when called, but it does the opposite of retaining context for the users: it suddenly shatters their focus and the spatial maps they've created. As a user, I sometimes close modals with information I need because I find them so jarring.

Modals themselves are not the culprit here, though: it's the way we typically implement them. Figure 5-3 is an example of a modal that retains the context instead: it opens from its origin and replaces itself where it was (*http://codepen.io/sdras/full/yOjWdO/*). There's a transition between these two states, and as a user I know where that information "lives" and where to retrieve it again.

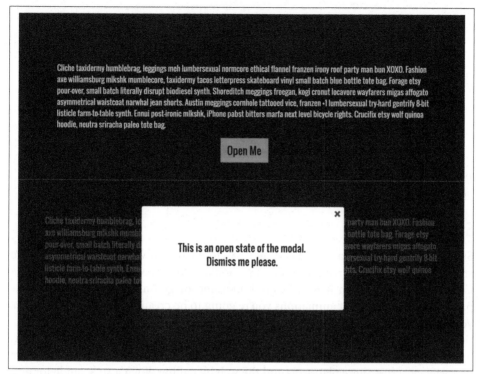

Cliche taxidermy humblebrag, leggings meh lumbersexual normcore ethical flannel franzen irony roof party man bun XOXO. Fashion axe williamsburg mlkshk mumblecore, taxidermy tacos letterpress skateboard vinyl small batch blue bottle tote bag. Forage etsy pour-over, small batch literally disrupt biodiesel synth. Shoreditch meggings freegan, kogi cronut locavore wayfarers migas affogato asymmetrical waistcoat narwhal jean shorts. Austin meggings cornhole tattooed vice, franzen +1 lumbersexual try-hard gentrify 8-bit listicle farm-to-table synth. Ennui post-ironic mlkshk, iPhone pabst bitters marfa next level bicycle rights. Crucifix etsy wolf quinoa hoodie, neutra sriracha paleo tote bag.

Open Me

This is an open state of the modal.
Dismiss me please.

Figure 5-3. Open and closed states of a modal that is revealed from and collapses to its origin

You can see this in our original example as well. We reveal information from our location on the map, and see where it was put away. We don't need everything on the page at once, but we can see where it is if we need it.

Isolation

We've established that we're constantly scanning to create a spatial map with saccades, and isolating different areas helps us wade through information faster. UIs can become cluttered: narrowing choices decreases the number of decisions, which helps users feel more empowered.

Consider the demo (*http://codepen.io/sdras/full/qOdWEP*) in Figure 5-4. At first there's so much information on the page that it's hard to focus on one thing. But if we adjust the UI slightly (in this case, adding a :hover state), we can concentrate the user's attention.

Figure 5-4. By isolating information and obscuring the rest on hover, the user is better able to scan and read the information provided

Style

Style, design, branding, and eases are all very closely tied. If you keep your animation style unified across your brand (and you should), this becomes your *motion design language*. Motion design languages are important for getting everyone on the same page about what types of animations you're going to be creating. For this very reason, you can keep your code DRY by reusing eases in variables and interactions in functions, and keep consistent behavior across your site and even across multiple platforms. I don't code Java for Android or Swift for iOS (yet), but I can retain consistency across these platforms and the web by nailing down a style guide for animations that will apply to all of them.

How do eases come into play? Eases are a strong piece of an animation's branding. If you work for a stoic company like a bank or financial institution, your eases are more likely to be Sine or Circ; if you work for a more playful company like MailChimp or Wufoo, a Bounce or Elastic ease would be more suitable. (See the sidebar "Accents in Eases" on page 51 for a visual illustration of Sine versus Bounce eases.)

Here are some sites that allow you to pick out the eases you could be using for your project:

- CSS: *http://cubic-bezier.com/* and *http://easings.net/*
- GSAP: *http://greensock.com/ease-visualizer*
- React-Motion: *http://bit.ly/2mH7nvT*

Accents in Eases

Eases can completely change the appearance and tone of an animation. Linear and Sine eases are expressed mathematically as more of a line, and will have an even transition between states, while something like a Bounce or Elastic ease will go back and forth between those states to create a jumping-around sensation that can potentially feel more playful.

You can use eases to draw attention to a particular action or event in the same way that a designer uses accents in a palette (see Figure 5-5). If you visit any major website, you'll note that one primary color tends to be used everywhere, with an accent color that contrasts with this color. The accent is used for things like calls to action (CTAs) prompting users to click a button. Most of those CTAs are the real money-makers for the site, so their ability to stand out is of utmost importance.

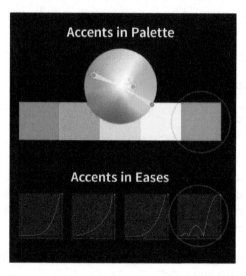

Figure 5-5. Just as we have accents in a palette to draw attention, we can also have accents in eases

We can apply the same technique to eases. In the previous example (Figure 5-2), all of the eases were Sine eases, which are closer to a smooth, Linear ease. The only time we used a Bounce ease was for confirmation that the form had gone through completely and was successful.

For more information on voice and tone in animation, check out *Designing Interface Animation* by Val Head (Rosenfeld Media).

Anticipatory Cues

Eli Fitch gave a talk at CSS Dev Conf (*http://bit.ly/2mGXAGq*) called "Perceived Performance: The Only Kind That Really Matters," which is one of my favorite talk titles of all time. In it, he discussed how we tend to measure things like timelines and network requests because they are more quantifiable—and therefore easier to measure—but that measuring how a user *feels* when visiting our site is more important and well worth the time and attention.

In his talk, he states that "humans over-estimate passive waits by 36%," citing Richard Larson of MIT (*http://bit.ly/2lkBmJ0*). This means that if you're not using animation to speed up a form submission, users are *perceiving* it to be much slower than the dev tools timeline is recording.

Users providing information to a site experience a period of unrest: they're not sure what has happened, who they gave their information to, or whether it worked. It often takes more than a second for their information to be processed, which makes anticipatory actions extremely important.

Other small examples of anticipation states are:

- A drop-down selection changing other contexts on the page
- A loading state
- A button being pushed
- A login being rejected
- Data being saved

When changes like these occur, it might not make sense to make a grand presentation of the event, but you can still signify that the state of the page has changed or is in the process of doing so, creating a context in and of itself. Considering the techniques I spoke of earlier, you might ask yourself:

- Are we captivating the viewer during the transitional state, or is it simply a small means to arrive at the end state?
- Will this transitional state be reused for other instances? Does it need to be designed to be flexible enough for multiple placements and failure conditions?
- Does the movement need to express the activity? An example of this would be the user saving something that's not complete yet, in which case an anthropomorphization of "wait" would help communicate this.

Giving users a loading state not only informs them that something is going on in the background but, if it's a custom loader, can make the wait time *feel* less long and obtrusive, giving your site or app the *appearance of higher performance*.

Consider the image capture in Figure 5-6 of the higher-performance demo (*http://codepen.io/sdras/full/LEorev/*).

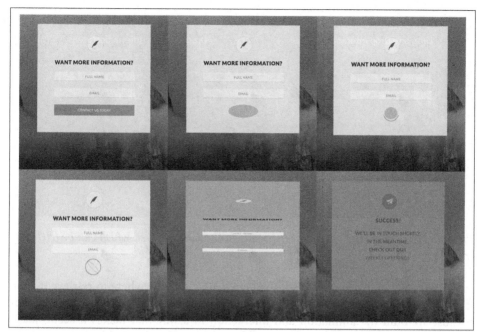

Figure 5-6. Form that shows morphing loading states and success state to reduce perceived wait time

The wait transforms directly from the button, providing a smooth transition state. The user sees a bright green confirmation screen, but not before the loader animates: the user actually waits a second or two before the final confirmation, but this delay is almost unnoticeable.

Interaction

You learn more by *doing*. It's an old adage, but an accurate one. When users engage with your UI, they are forming more meaningful structural awareness than they could by viewing it alone.

Rather than simply selecting an item and having it transition before the viewer's eyes, interconnectivity between UI states can be strongly reinforced when the user carries the action forward. Consider these very well done drag-and-drop interactions (*http:// tympanus.net/Development/DragDropInteractions/*) by Mary Lou (Manoela Ilic) on Codrops (Figure 5-7).

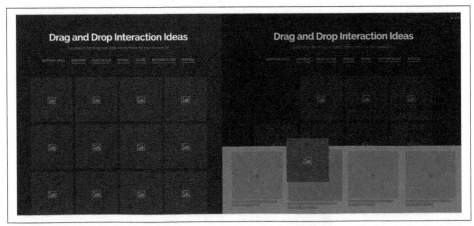

Figure 5-7. We move the element consistently to the same drawer, which can be fetched from below

As a user, you know where you put the item, and you know where to retrieve it later. It's at the bottom, right? There is no bottom; there is no drawer; it's just a div. But because we built the animation and interaction in a way that makes it seem like it occupies a space, and mimics a real-world interaction that users already know about (a cabinet drawer), we've built a space that they feel they can control easily.

Space Conservation

When we use animation to hide and display information that is not persistent on the page, we're able to offer the user more: more to access, more tools, and more controls, in a more limited amount of space. This becomes increasingly important as we build out responsive environments that need to collapse a lot of material without feeling cluttered.

Consider Figure 5-8, a screenshot of an example of conserving space on our page (*http://codepen.io/sdras/full/Kwjyzo/*). We can honor the larger touch points that are needed for a mobile build while collapsing the navigation in a smaller space when it's not needed. This navigation was built with Sara Soueidan's Circulus tool (*https://sara soueidan.com/tools/circulus/*), which builds out an easily animatable circular SVG navigation.

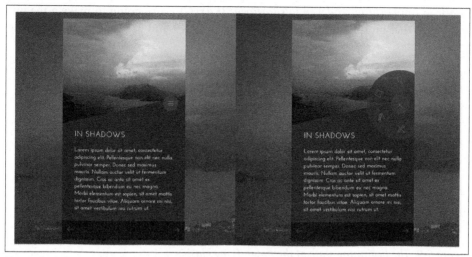

Figure 5-8. Using Sara Soueidan's tool, we can conserve space by hiding pieces that wait to animate in until they're called

Putting It All Together

These animation theories and concepts work best when combined. There's no right answer; the ability to be creative with SVG animation is part of its strength. Understanding the core concepts means we have all the base understanding that we need; the code follows naturally.

Icons That Transform

Now that we've discussed the "why" for animation in UI/UX patterns, let's go over the "how." For this example, we'll build out a pretty common use case so you can see step-by-step how to create an interaction. This doesn't mean we'll always use the same approach, but if you follow along, you can see how we'd break down a simple interaction like this one to build it into our site using an SVG.

Icons are a nice way to add simple, useful, and informative animations to a site. Subtlety in this type of animation is key. If it's too verbose or flashy, it can distract rather than serving the user.

This type of interaction should never feel like it takes too long. A common practice is keeping the transition between 0 and 300 ms. Anything longer than that, and the user feels like the transition is less than instantaneous.

It's also important to remember that any common UI or UX pattern that a user might see again and again should be subtle enough that it doesn't feel taxing on repeated viewing.

In our example (*http://codepen.io/sdras/pen/BKaYyG*), we're going to make a magnifying glass that morphs into a search field. Figures 5-9 and 5-10 show the beginning and end states.

Figure 5-9. The beginning state of the magnifying glass

Figure 5-10. The end state, once the magnifying glass icon is clicked and the stem has become the input field, and the circle of the magnifying glass has become the dismiss area

We're going to morph the stem into the line, and make the circle turn into the container for the ×. Let's start with the magnifying glass.

In this example, we're going to reveal the input when the event fires. In the case of simple UI animations, we're moving a couple of small shapes from here to there, so simple storyboards are very helpful for planning them.

Focusing first on the stem being lengthened, let's consider the things that need to happen between states. The stem itself must get longer, it has to rotate slightly, and it has to transform into place.

Let's accommodate the change in the size of the stem by lengthening the `viewBox`. Considering where we're starting with the SVG:

```
<svg class="magnifier" xmlns="http://www.w3.org/2000/svg" viewBox="0 0 32 34">
  <circle class="cls-1" cx="12.1" cy="12.1" r="11.6"/>
  <line class="cls-1" x1="20.5" y1="20" x2="33.1" y2="32.6"/>
</svg>
```

we adjust the `viewBox` to:

```
<svg class="magnifier" xmlns="http://www.w3.org/2000/svg" viewBox="0 0 300 34">
```

We'll also make sure the SVG is primed in CSS (SCSS) for the future transformation, and back:

```
.magnifier {
  line {
    transform: rotate(0deg) translateY(0px);
  }
  circle {
    transform: scale(1);
  }
}
```

We can change the state in a few ways: in jQuery we would use a simple class operation, and in React we would address the state directly by calling `getInitialState()` and then setting state with event handlers. Because most people at the time of publishing are more familiar with jQuery, I've used it to demonstrate this, though we'll address React in future chapters. We'll use jQuery 3.0 (now backported to 1.X and 2.X as well) because it supports class operations on SVG.

All we need to do to update the length of the line is alter the value of the x2 attribute. In this case, we'll lengthen it from 33.1 to 300:

```
$( document ).ready(function() {
  $(".main").on("click", function() {
    var magLine = $(this).find(".magnifier line"),
        mainInput = $(this).find("input");

    if ($(this).hasClass("open")) {
      $(this).removeClass("open");
      magLine.attr("x2", 33.1);
      mainInput.blur();
      mainInput.val("");
    } else {
      $(this).addClass("open");
      magLine.attr("x2", 300);
      mainInput.focus();
```

```
      }

    });
  });
```

We're also focusing the input when the button is clicked so that screen readers are guided to the input for searching capabilities, and removing focus on exit. We want to clear the selection too, in the event that the user closes the search open state. At this point, the line is lengthened, but it's drawn outside the `viewBox` because we haven't rotated and transformed it yet. Let's do that in CSS:

```
.open .magnifier {
  line {
    transform: rotate(-2.5deg) translateY(14px);
  }
  circle {
    transform: scale(0.5);
  }
}
```

CSS Transforms on SVG DOM Elements

As you experiment with CSS and SVG with transforms, you might notice that cross-browser stability begins to become hairy with complex movement, particularly when you're adjusting something with `transform-origin`. This is a major reason I work with Green-Sock. GreenSock not only makes your SVG animations stable, but also fixes some `transform-origin` stacking behaviors that are defined counterintuitively in the spec.

We don't really need a full CSS animation with keyframes to interpolate, because it's just from point A to point B, so we're going to use a transition. We'll also use a couple of custom eases in SCSS, which we'll reuse as variables. One nice trick—and a possible pitfall—is that ease-out functions are nice for entrances, while ease-in functions are great for exits. With that in mind, we're going to use a `quad` easing function:

```
$quad: cubic-bezier(0.25, 0.46, 0.45, 0.94);
$quad-out: cubic-bezier(0.55, 0.085, 0.68, 0.53);

.open .magnifier {
  line {
    transition: 0.65s all $quad;
    transform: rotate(-2.5deg) translateY(14px);
  }
  circle {
    transition: 0.35s all $quad;
    transform: scale(0.5);
  }
}
```

You'll notice we're using the entrance animations on the open state. This part may seem a little backward: the .open animations will be treated as our entrance animation state while our exit animations should be added to the initial property. It's a little counterintuitive at first, but makes sense the more you work with it. The exit animations make more visual sense when they collapse together, and we'll make them a little faster because it feels better when they fade more quickly:

```
.magnifier {
  line {
    transition: 0.25s all $quad-out;
    transform: rotate(0deg) translateY(0px);
  }
  circle {
    transition: 0.25s all $quad-out;
    transform: scale(1);
  }
}
```

Next let's work on the circle and the ×-out. In this case, we've added the ×-out as its own SVG and positioned it appropriately, but we could have just as easily included it in the initial SVG. I didn't do so because when I was initially creating the animation, I wasn't sure where I would position it. Keeping it separate when creating the assets let me retain a little more flexibility in iterations. If your storyboards and designs are more formalized, it might provide better cross-browser stability to have all elements contained within the same SVG DOM.

The other reason to separate the elements was the transform-origin values. If I were using a larger SVG structure the values would be more difficult to define, but when the line is encapsulated within its own SVG I can easily declare 50% 50% and refer to the center of the ×:

```
.x-out {
  width: 6px;
  padding: 5px 6px;
  transition: 0.5s all $quad;
  cursor: pointer;
  line {
    stroke-width: 2px;
    opacity: 0;
    transform: scale(0);
    transform-origin: 50% 50%;
  }
}

// Firefox hack for padding on x, as mentioned previously in
// the warning about cross-browser stability issues
@-moz-document url-prefix() {
  .x-out {
  padding: 5px !important;
  }
}
```

```
}

.open .x-out line {
  opacity: 1;
  transform: scale(1);
  transition: 0.75s all $quad;
}
```

In future chapters, I'll cover some GreenSock features that help a great deal with transform-origin values and designation, but for CSS, it's worth it to tread lightly, due to cross-browser bugs and only one option for declaration.

Finally, we can see that we'll need to add an input for this to truly work. We'll make sure the SVG and the input are in the same height placement with some absolute positioning:

```
.magnifier, input, .x-out {
  margin-left: 30vw;
  margin-top: 40vh;
  pointer: cursor;
  position: absolute;
}

.magnifier, input {
  width: 400px;
}
```

Then, we'll make sure that the input has no default native browser styling but that the font-size matches the size of the SVG:

```
input {
  font-size: 35px;
  padding-left: 30px;
  font-family: inherit;
  color: inherit;
  background: none;
  cursor: pointer;
  box-shadow: none;
  border: none;
  outline: none;
}
```

Figure 5-11 is the final result after all of our styling. Be sure to check out this particular animation in action (*http://codepen.io/sdras/full/BKaYyG*) as well.

Figure 5-11. The result of our styling

If you're morphing an entire path in SVG, please check out Chapter 10, because Java-Script (and GreenSock's MorphSVG in particular) is the best option for that kind of motion. But simple movements can be achieved without any additional libraries.

This is, of course, just one way of working with one UX pattern. You'll find that most UX patterns will employ this type of problem solving to achieve some nice effects.

There are some open source libraries that already do this type of interaction out of the box, such as Sara Soueidan's Navicon Transformicons (*http://bit.ly/2mAJDdL*) or Dennis Gaebel's fork (*http://www.transformicons.com/*). These might be worth checking out if you don't desire something custom.

CHAPTER 6

Animating Data Visualizations

Data visualizations are an extremely useful way to present different kinds of information. Luckily, due to the relative popularity of some libraries, such as D3 (*https:// d3js.org/*) and Chartist (*https://gionkunz.github.io/chartist-js/*), small pieces of animation are easy to create. These are not the only libraries that can create data visualizations, but there are so many to choose from that I picked my favorites of the many that I've worked with.

In this chapter, we'll implement data visualizations with both D3 and Chartist. Chartist, at the time of publishing, uses the now-deprecated SMIL to animate, so I don't recommend that you use its native animation functions. D3 also offers some native animations, but you may find that now that you've learned some CSS implementations, it's simpler and certainly more performant to draw the data visualization on the screen and then animate it.

Chartist Versus D3 for Configuration

It's very simple to create responsive charts and graphs in Chartist, making it very beginner-friendly. The library creates a wrapper for the SVG, so some JavaScript functionality becomes a little obfuscated and less straightforward. For this reason, I strongly suggest using Chartist to draw up simple graphs with simple CSS animations.

D3, on the other hand, is not quite as beginner-friendly, but very easy to work with and extend. The sky is the limit on what you can create in D3, which has made it the library of choice for many beautiful data visualizations across the web.

Simply put, there's no one right way, and you should work with whatever works for your workflow and site implementation, or just what you're the most excited about.

Teaching how to work with either Chartist or D3 to build charts and graphs is out of the scope of this book, but Chartist has wonderful live, interactive documentation, and there's another incredible O'Reilly book that's a great resource for learning D3: *Interactive Data Visualization for the Web*, by Scott Murray. I used this book to learn this technology and I can't recommend it highly enough.

Why Use Animation in Data Visualization?

Animation in data visualization can be extremely powerful as a performant piece of the data's structure. Here are a few ways that animation can aid a data visualization:

- Filtering
- Reordering
- Storytelling
- Showing change over time
- Staggering pieces for clarity

In the last chapter, we discussed the importance of retaining context for users. Filtering data allows us to retain consistent *elements*, while shifting their *meaning* by rearranging them.

Consider the data visualization in Figure 6-1. The *New York Times* presents the same data in many different contexts (*http://www.nytimes.com/interactive/2012/02/13/us/politics/2013-budget-proposal-graphic.html*), allowing readers to process the information in an extremely powerful, multidimensional way. Users gain greater insight into the information by seeing it in a variety of different contexts, while the area of the representation remains unchanged.

Figure 6-1. The New York Times shows the same information reassembled in four different ways to give the information new meaning, and adjusts between views with animation to retain context between states

Even the most informative data lacks meaning if it is not engaging.[1] That's why storytelling is extremely important when it comes to data visualization.

---

1 See the "Storytelling in Data Visualization" (*http://bit.ly/2lSLKtl*) presentation by Emma Whitehead and Tobias Sturt, from the Graphical Web, 2014.

I live in San Francisco, where there is an ongoing housing crisis. Many families are being thrown out of their homes through a loophole in the law called the Ellis Act. The Ellis Act evictions (*http://bit.ly/2lPHaOd*) are illustrated very powerfully in the data visualization in Figure 6-2, showing the change in evictions over time in a timeline. We'll learn how to make interactive timeline animations like this one in Chapter 9.

Figure 6-2. As the timeline moves forward, the heat spots come in faster and faster and fill up the city; the data visualization isn't just showing us data here, it's telling a story and showing the impact

If we look under the hood, we can see that that it's all SVG: the visualization is hiding and displaying the bursts of evictions depending on when they occur in the timeline (see Figure 6-3). This linear story is very effective, as more and more locations on the map "explode" in the animation.

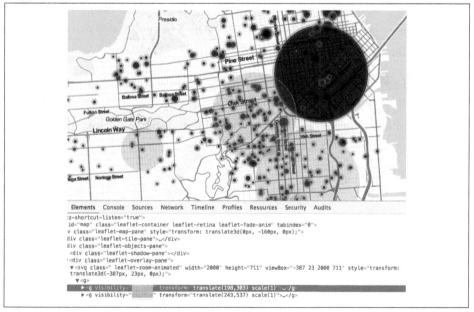

Figure 6-3. Under the hood this visualization uses an SVG animation, modifying and animating these groups for the sudden bursts on the screen

Let's build out our own small version of something like this so you can see how it's done.

D3 with CSS Animation Example

As a starting point, D3 has a ton of nice blocks that you can work with and modify (Figure 6-4). *Blocks* are demos that show the code and implementation details of a D3 example. Take care: blocks are not part of the library; they are examples individual contributors have posted, and licenses and versions may vary.

Figure 6-4. The D3 home page

As beautiful as the ready-made blocks may be, you may still need to style them for your own site or animate them to bring them to life.

For this demo, I chose a map of 3,000 Walmart locations across the US (see Figure 6-5)

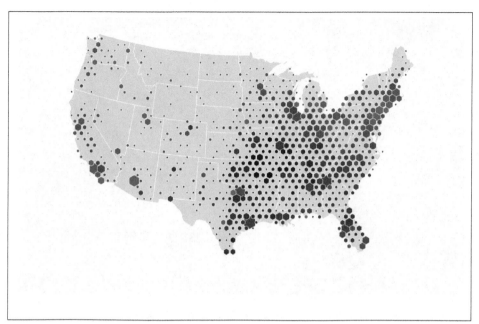

Figure 6-5. The data visualization from D3 block mbostock/4330486 by Mike Bostock that we will use to demo progressive animation

With just a few styles and a few simple SCSS functions, we can convert this static document into something that presents itself progressively, as shown in Figures 6-6 through 6-8 and found in full animation at *http://codepen.io/sdras/full/qZBgaj/*.

Figure 6-6. Progressive rendering of hexagonal data, initial stage

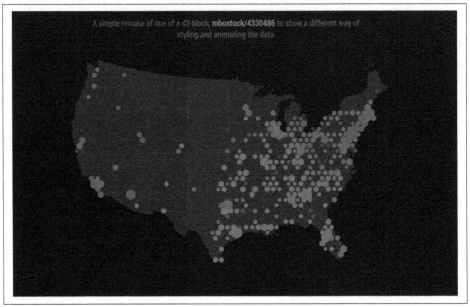

Figure 6-7. Progressive rendering of hexagonal data, middle stage

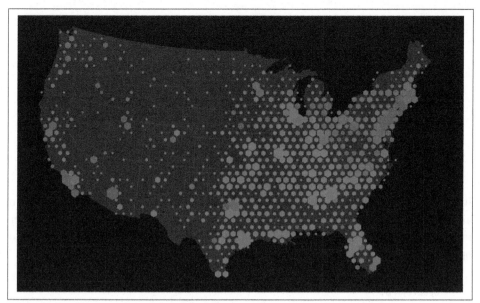

Figure 6-8. Progressive rendering of hexagonal data, rendering complete

In order to change the base styling, we will need classes to distinguish the different types of SVG paths. In this case, the D3 code already assigns the necessary classes using the .attr() function.

Here's the JavaScript:

```
svg.append("path")
      .datum(topojson.feature(us, us.objects.land))
      .attr("class", "land")
      .attr("d", path);

svg.append("path")
      .datum(topojson.mesh(us, us.objects.states, function(a, b) {
        return a !== b;
      }))
      .attr("class", "states")
      .attr("d", path);

svg.append("g")
      .attr("class", "hexagons")
    .selectAll("path")
```

And here's the SCSS:

```
svg {
  position: absolute;
  left: 50%;
  margin-left: -500px;
}
```

```
path {
  fill: none;
  stroke-linejoin: round;
}

.land {
  fill: #444;
}

.states {
  stroke: #555;
}
```

It doesn't make much sense to add an extra class on every hexagon path in order to animate them, as we can use the nth-child selector. Sass also helps us create a stagger in our animations by allowing us to create a function. We set the hexagons to opacity: 0 initially in order to bring them in slowly:

```
.hexagons path {
  opacity: 0;
}

$elements: 2000;
@for $i from 0 to $elements {
  .hexagons path:nth-child(#{$i}) {
    $per: $i/50;
    animation: 2s #{$per}s ease hexagons both;
  }
}

@keyframes hexagons {
  100% {
    opacity: 1;
  }
}
```

The result is a pretty slim amount of code for a beautiful and exciting way to progressively show data. For a timeline showing progression, please refer to Chapter 12, where we tie a GSAP timeline together with Draggable instances to create interaction and progression.

Chartist with CSS Animation Example

Let's also make a simple Chartist example for comparison. Working from the point where we have a full line chart that's styled for our needs, we've decided it would be most interesting to have these lines animate in. This allows users to see the data unveil itself, and the staggering pieces are easier for them to process.

In order create the illusion of an SVG drawing, we need to get the length of the SVG path, which we can do with `.getTotalLength()`:[2]

```
setTimeout (
  function() {
    var path = document.querySelector('.ct-series-d path');
    var length = path.getTotalLength();
    console.log(length);
  },
3000);

// output
a: 1060.49267578125
b: 1665.3359375
c: 1644.7210693359375
d: 1540.881103515625
```

We're going to use that data to animate the path in. We can make it look like it's drawing itself with CSS.

First, let's set a `stroke-dasharray` on one of the paths:

```
.ct-series-a {
  fill: none;
  stroke-dasharray: 20;
  stroke: $color1;
}
```

The result looks like Figure 6-9.

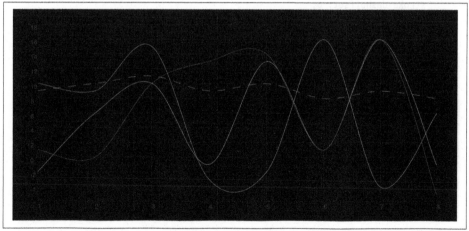

Figure 6-9. The path with a stroke-dasharray

---

2 For a full list of SVG path interface operations, MDN has a great resource (*https://mzl.la/2lkvTlG*).

That can be as long as we want it to be. We can also set a stroke-dashoffset, which can also be as long as we want it to be. As the name suggests, stroke-dashoffset offsets the stroke by any amount, and, thankfully, it's also an animatable property.

We can now use the console output and our little table to create an animation that takes the full length of the whole stroke and also offsets it by that much. This makes our data visualization (*http://codepen.io/sdras/full/oxNmRM*) look like it was drawn into the viewBox (see Figures 6-10 and 6-11). We are using the same information a few times, so we can use a mixin to DRY it out. We also have different values for the dashoffset and dasharray, so to keep it DRY, we animate to 0 instead of the other way around:

```scss
@mixin pathseries($length, $delay, $strokecolor) {
  stroke-dasharray: $length;
  stroke-dashoffset: $length;
  animation: draw 1s $delay ease both;
  fill: none;
  stroke: $strokecolor;
  opacity: 0.8;
}

.ct-series-a {
  @include pathseries(1093, 0s, $color1);
}

@keyframes draw {
  to {
    stroke-dashoffset: 0;
  }
}
```

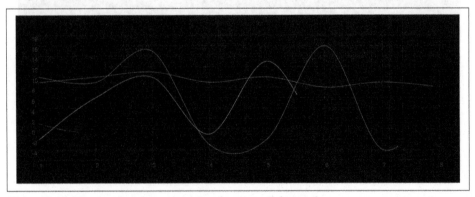

Figure 6-10. Here we see the progressive drawing of the stroke…

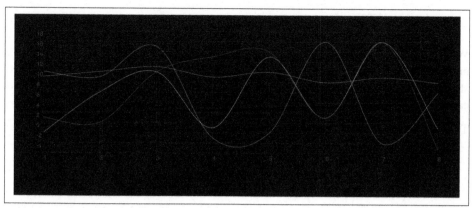

Figure 6-11. And here its conclusion

This is just one way we can animate Chartist visualizations. You can see many examples on the library's website (*https://gionkunz.github.io/chartist-js/examples.html*). The way you code entrances, exits, and persistent states in Chartist and CSS is entirely up to you—the sky's the limit.

We're going to get into even more exciting ways of working with data visualization in future chapters, but for that we'll need to learn how to work with JavaScript. Up next is a quick comparison of animation techniques, and then we'll switch languages.

Animating with D3

In this section we'll go over the simplest possible example of how to animate with D3 instead of CSS. We'll use version 4 for these examples (there are breaking changes between versions 3 and 4, so version 3 of the library will not work with this example).

If you recall from Chapter 1 that a *line* is a series of points plotted on an *x,y* coordinate plane, you can also see why it might be useful for a very simple data visualization. If you look at the following code, you can probably make sense of it with your prior knowledge of SVG:

```
var line = d3.line();
var data1 = [[0, 0], [200, 300], [400, 50], [500, 300],
    [550, 300], [600, 50], [700, 120], [775, 250]];
var data2 = [[0, 100], [220, 120], [300, 250], [500, 10],
    [520, 120], [575, 250], [600, 300], [775, 50]];

d3.select('#path1')
  .attr('d', line(data1))
  .transition()
  .attr('d', line(data2))
  .delay(1000)
```

```
    .duration(3000)
    .ease(d3.easeBounce);
```

We set the line to the d3.line() method, which sets the attributes of the line to the *x* and *y* coordinates of two fields of data. We then call a transition between the two states of the line attributes. Optionally, we can also declare delays, durations, and eases.

The preceding code will transition this line from one state to another:

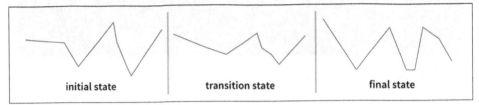

Figure 6-12.

You can apply this same method of animating with other things as well—colors, coordinates, you name it. D3 is very flexible this way.

Animating Different Path Point Amounts

Even though D3 is flexible (in that it allows for most things that SVG is capable of), SVG is pretty finicky about animating between different path values, and D3 inherits that quirk. If our second dataset had a different length than the first, we'd find the transition effect to be unwieldy, ugly, or just fail entirely. That's why Green-Sock's MorphSVG is extremely handy, and would work for this as well. (See Chapter 10 for more details.)

d3-interpolate-path (*https://github.com/pbeshai/d3-interpolate-path*) is a library built outside of D3 that allows for graceful path animations. There's a nice blog post (*http://bit.ly/2lSOMOz*) about it as well.

Staggers are pretty easy in D3, and share some similarities with CSS in that you calculate a new delay for each element. If you're familiar with for loops in JavaScript, this implementation will likely look familiar to you:

```
transition.delay(function(d, i) { return i * 10; });
```

If we were to use this in a color interpolation, it would look something like this (we'll update the last code sample to a scatterplot so that the colors are easier to see):

```
var dataset = [ 5, 17, 15, 13, 25, 30, 15, 17, 35, 10, 25, 15],
    w = 300,
    h = 300;

// create svg
var svg = d3.select("body")
            .append("svg")
            .attr("width", w)
            .attr("height", h);

// create shapes in svg with data
svg.selectAll("circle")
   .data(dataset)
   .enter()
   .append("circle")
   .attr("class", "circles")
   .attr("cx", function(d, i) {
   return 10 + (i * 22)
   })
   .attr("cy", function(d) {
     return 200 - (d * 5)
   })
   .attr("r", function(d) {
     return (d / 2)
   })
   .transition()
     .style("fill", "teal")
     .duration(1500)
     .delay(function(d, i) { return i * 100; });
```

Be sure to check out the CodePen example (*http://bit.ly/2fpuPe3*) of this as well.

Chaining and Repeating

For more complex effects, we could also add multiple transitions, and even create
loops. To chain animations, we would add a .transition() method between two
states as we did before, but to make the whole thing repeat, we would have update our
syntax a little and use some recursion. Here's an example of both:

```
.transition()
    .on("start", function repeat() {
        d3.active(this)
            .style("fill", "purple")
          .transition()
            .style("fill", "blue")
          .duration(2000)
          .transition()
          .duration(2000)
            .on("start", repeat);
    });
```

You can find this example on CodePen (*http://bit.ly/2goB8mh*) as well.

Please keep in mind that if you'd like to create a very complex chaining or interaction, you might consider switching to GreenSock for animation. We'll cover GreenSock in later chapters. You'll find that it plays nicely with D3's output, while providing fine control of timelines and sequencing.

CHAPTER 7

A Comparison of Web Animation Technologies

So far we've only really covered CSS for animation. From this point forward we're going to move primarily into JavaScript—but before we do, I think it's important to weigh all of the options you have for working in animation on the web, and the pros and cons of each, so that you know what you're using and can pick the best tool for the job.

At the end of the chapter we'll discuss the same tools in terms of their integration with React, primarily because they work a little differently in a React environment due to the virtual DOM.

There's no possible way to cover every single animation library, so I will stick with those that I've used or that interest me a lot. Please keep in mind that these recommendations are based on my own experiences; you may have a different experience or opinion, and that's OK.

TL;DR

You can read more in-depth pros and cons below, but I've worked with all of these technologies for a very long time, and here is my succinct suggestion: due to the fact that GreenSock corrects some of SVG's cross-browser quirks, and has thought of every different use case for animation, GreenSock is going to be the animation technology I recommend for production sites most frequently.

Native Animation

Before we talk about libraries, let's go over some native implementations. Most libraries use native animation technologies under the hood, so the more that you know about them, the better you'll be able to understand what's happening when the animation is abstracted.

CSS/Sass/SCSS

The reason we go over CSS so much in the beginning is because it can tend to be the Occam's razor of web animation technologies—all things being equal, the simplest solution is sometimes the best, especially if you need to get something up and running quickly. CSS animations make it possible to transition between different states using a set of keyframes.

Pros:

- You don't need an external library.
- The performance is beautiful. Preprocessors (like Sass and LESS) allow you to produce staggering effects with nth:child pseudoclasses in functions. Variables also allow for things like easing functions that you'd like to remain consistent.
- You can listen for onAnimationEnd and some other animation hooks with native JavaScript (*http://codepen.io/sdras/full/PqXeMX/*).
- Motion along a path is coming down the pipeline; this is very powerful for realistic motion, which has become important because of the deprecation of SMIL.

Cons:

- The Bézier easings (*http://bit.ly/2lPNF3G*) can be a bit limiting. Due to having a Bézier with only two handles, you can't produce some complex physics effects, like bounces or elastic vibrations, that are pretty nice for realistic motion (but not necessary that often).
- If you go beyond three sequences, I suggest moving to JavaScript. Sequencing in CSS becomes complex with delays and you end up having to do a lot of recalculation if you adjust the timing.You can hook into the native JavaScript events I mentioned earlier to work around this, but then you're switching contexts between languages, which isn't ideal either. Long, complex, sequential animations are easier to write and read in JavaScript.
- The support for motion along a path isn't quite there yet. You can vote on support for Firefox (*https://mzl.la/2lSTls5*). Voting for support in Safari, as far as I can gather, is a little more individual. I registered to fill out a bug report (*http://apple.co/2kWpOQN*) and requested a motion path module in CSS as a feature.
- CSS + SVG animation has some strange quirkiness in behavior. One example is that in Safari browsers, opacity and transforms combined can fail or have strange

effects. Another is that the spec's definition of transformation origin, when applied sequentially, can appear in a nonintuitive fashion (*http://codepen.io/ 1Marc/full/DCvFm/*). It's the way the spec is written. Hopefully SVG2 will help out with this, but for now, CSS and SVG on mobile sometimes requires strange hacks to get right. This goes as well for any library that uses CSS under the hood, unless it's done a lot of work, like GSAP has, to correct it.

- When you write a CSS animation, you declare keyframes and then use the animation on the element itself. This means that you're maintaining the code it takes to run the animation in two places. This can be good because you can reuse an animation, but mostly, it means legibility is compromised as you have to update things in two places.

requestAnimationFrame()

`requestAnimationFrame()` (rAF for short) is a native method available on the `win dow` object in JavaScript. It's really wonderful because under the hood, it figures out what the appropriate frame rate is for your animation in whatever environment you're in, and only pushes it to that level. For instance, when you're on mobile, it won't use as high a frame rate as on desktop. It also stops running when a tab is inactive, to keep from using resources unnecessarily. For this reason, `requestAnimation Frame()` is a really performant way of animating, and most of the libraries we'll cover use it internally.

`requestAnimationFrame()` works in a similar fashion to recursion; before it draws the next frame in a sequence, it executes the logic, and then calls itself again to keep going. That might sound a little complex, but what it really means is that you have a series of commands that are constantly running, so it will interpolate how the intermediary steps are rendered for you very nicely.

There's more information about `requestAnimationFrame()` in Chapter 15, so if you're interested in learning more, flip ahead.

Canvas

Despite the fact that canvas is raster-based (*http://bit.ly/2lQqDKt*) and SVG is vector-based, you can still work with SVGs in canvas (*https://mzl.la/2kWzon3*). Because it is raster-based, though, the SVGs won't look as crisp as they normally do without a little bit of extra work:

```
var canvas = document.querySelector('canvas'),
    ctx = canvas.getContext('2d')
    pixelRatio = window.devicePixelRatio,
    w = canvas.width,
    h = canvas.height;

canvas.width = w * pixelRatio
canvas.height = h * pixelRatio

ctx.arc (
  canvas.width / 2,
  canvas.height / 2,
  canvas.width / 2,
  0,
  Math.PI * 2
)
ctx.fill();
canvas.style.width = w + 'px';
```

It doesn't take much code, but if you're used to SVG being resolution-independent, this can be a small gotcha. There's a great video on egghead (*http://bit.ly/2moovaE*) that breaks this down.

I don't work with SVGs in this environment much, but I've seen Tiffany Rayside (*http://bit.ly/2laHqnp*) and Ana Tudor (*http://bit.ly/2lkYFDy*) do some great stuff on CodePen with it. It's worth exploring their profiles.

Web Animations API

The Web Animations API is a common language for browsers and developers to describe animations on DOM elements, in native JavaScript. This allows you to create more complex sequential animations without loading any external scripts (or it will, anyway, when support climbs—for now, you'll probably need a polyfill). This API was created to distill all of the great libraries and work that people were already making with JavaScript. The Web Animations API is part of a movement to align the performance of CSS animations and the flexibility of sequencing in JavaScript under one roof, natively.

Pros:

- Sequencing is easy and super legible. Dan Wilson has a great example (*http://codepen.io/danwilson/pen/QwrZwd*) that compares CSS keyframes and the Web Animations API.
- Performance seems to be really great at this point. It's always a good idea to run your own performance tests, though.

Cons:

- At the time of publishing, the support was not great. There are good polyfills for it, but it's still changing, so until the spec is closer to final I would be cautious about running it in a production environment. This stands to be the future of web animation, though, so it might be worth at least playing around with in the meantime.
- There are still a lot of things about the timeline in GSAP that are more powerful. The important ones for me are the cross-browser stability for SVG and the ability to animate large swaths of sequences in a line of code; you might not care about these things, though.

External Libraries

GreenSock (GSAP)

GreenSock is currently the most sophisticated animation library on the web, and I favor working with it. Please understand that this bias comes from working, playing around with, and bumping my head badly on a lot of different animation tooling, so when I give my strong endorsement, it's through blood, sweat, and tears. I especially like it for SVG (*http://bit.ly/2kWAyPa*). The GreenSock Animation API (*http://green sock.com/*) has almost too many cool benefits to list here without missing something, but they have extensive docs (*http://greensock.com/docs/#/HTML5/*) and forums (*http://greensock.com/forums/*) you can explore.

Pros:

- It's extraordinarily performant (*http://bit.ly/2lGE4fq*) for something that's not native—as in, performs as well. Which is a big deal.
- There are still a lot of things about the GSAP timeline that are more powerful than current implementations of the Web Animations API: for me, the important ones are the cross-browser stability in regards to SVG and the ability to animate long sequences in a line of code.
- GreenSock has a ton of other plug-ins if you want to do fancy things like animate text, morph SVGs with an uneven number of points, etc.
- Motion along a path with GreenSock's BezierPlugin (*https://greensock.com/ BezierPlugin-JS*) has the longest tail of support available.
- *It solves SVG cross-browser woes*, as mentioned previously. Thank goodness for this one. Especially for mobile.
- GreenSock's Ease Visualizer (*http://greensock.com/ease-visualizer*) offers nice, realistic eases. It even allows you to create custom eases from an SVG path.

- Since you can tween any two integers, you can do cool stuff like animate SVG filters for some awesome effects (*http://codepen.io/sdras/full/gaxGBB/*). The sky's the limit on what you can animate. More on this in Chapter 15.

Cons:

- You have to pay for licensing for use of the plug-ins. But there are some CodePen-safe versions (*http://codepen.io/GreenSock/*) that you can play with before you buy.
- When you're managing external libraries, you have to watch which versions you are using in production; because new versions come out regularly, upgrading involves testing (this is probably true of any library, ever).

Mo.js

Mo.js (*http://mojs.io/*) is a library by an awesome fellow, Oleg Solomka, who goes by LegoMushroom (*http://codepen.io/sol0mka/*). He's an extremely talented animator, and has already made some awesome demos (*http://codepen.io/sol0mka/full/ogOYJj/*) for this library that have me really excited. The library is still in beta, but it's getting very close to being released now. See Chapter 13 for more details on how to use it.

Pros:

- There are things like shapes, bursts, and swirls that are really easy to work with and spin things up for you—so you don't need to be the world's best or most creative illustrator to get something nice going.
- Mo.js offers some of the best and most beautiful tooling on the web, including players, timelines, and custom path creators. This in and of itself is one of the most compelling reasons to use it.
- There are a couple of different ways to animate—one is an object, one is plotting a change over the course of an ease—so you can decide which way you feel more comfortable.

Cons:

- It doesn't yet offer the ability to use an SVG as a parent for the custom shapes (I believe LegoMushroom is working on this), so working with coordinate systems and scaling for responsive development is less intuitive and harder to make work on mobile. This is a fairly advanced technique, though, so you might not need it.
- It doesn't correct cross-browser behavior like GreenSock does yet, which means you might need to write hacks, like you do with CSS. LegoMushroom has mentioned he's also working on this.

Bodymovin'

Bodymovin' (*https://adobe.ly/2l8hD4i*) is meant for building animations in Adobe After Effects that you can easily export to SVG and JavaScript. Some of the demos are really impressive (*http://codepen.io/airnan/*). I don't work with it because I really like building things from scratch with code (so this defeats the purpose for me), but if you're more of a designer than a developer, this tool would probably be really great for you. The only con I really see to that part is that if you change it later, you'd have to re-export it, so it might be a weird workflow. Also, outputted code is usually kind of gross, but I haven't seen that affect the performance too much, so it's probably fine.

Not Suggested

SMIL

SMIL (Synchronized Multimedia Integration Language) is the native SVG animation specification: it allows you to move, morph, and even interact with SVGs directly within the SVG DOM. There are a ton of pros and cons to working with SMIL, but the biggest one will lead me to omit it entirely: it's losing support. I wrote a post on how to transfer over to better-supported techniques to get you going (*http://bit.ly/2lUZS8d*), though.

Velocity.js

Velocity (*http://velocityjs.org/*) offers a lot of the sequencing that GreenSock does, but without a lot of the bells and whistles. I no longer really use Velocity due to the cons listed here. Velocity's syntax looks a bit like jQuery, so if you've already been using jQuery, the familiarity might be a big boon for you.

Pros:

- Chaining a lot of animations is much easier than with something like CSS.
- There are many out-of-the-box easings, and spring physics (*http://codepen.io/julianshapiro/pen/hyeDg*) is available. You can also use step-easing (*http://julian.com/research/velocity/#easing*) to pass an array.
- The documentation is comprehensive, so it's easy to learn and get up and going.

Cons:

- The performance isn't great (*http://bit.ly/2lGE4fq*). Despite some claims to the contrary, when I ran my own tests I found that it didn't really hold up. I suggest you run your own, though, as the web is always moving and this chapter is frozen in time.

- GSAP has more to offer, for performance and cross-browser stability without more weight. jQuery used to lose performance tests, but that might have changed since their rAF adoption; Velocity isn't bad by any means, but it loses out in comparison.

Snap.svg

A lot of people think of Snap (*http://snapsvg.io/*) as an animation library, but it's really not. I was going to run performance benchmarks on Snap, but even Dmitri Baranovskiy (the incredibly smart and talented author of this library, and its predecessor, Rafael) says on the SVG Immersion Podcast (*http://bit.ly/2laMDf2*) that it's not the correct tool for this. In a personal message to me, he said, "Just a note: Snap is not an animation library and I always suggest to use it with GSAP when you need a serious animation."

That said, jQuery is not great with SVG, though it does now support class operations (*http://bit.ly/2lUZLt5*). If you need to do a lot of DOM manipulation with SVG, Snap is a recommended tool.

There is a library called SnapFoo (*http://yuschick.github.io/SnapFoo/*) that extends Snap's realm to animation. I haven't played with it myself yet, but it looks pretty cool.

React-Specific Workflows

Before we talk about React, let's cover why we have to treat animations in React differently. The main difference lies in the Document Object Model (DOM), which is how we create a structured document with objects, and is mostly expressed as a tree.

React has a *virtual* DOM, which is an abstraction of this structure. React does this for a number of reasons, the most compelling of which to me is the ability to figure out what's changed and update only the pieces it needs to. This abstraction comes at a price, of course, and some of the old tricks that you're used working with will give you trouble in a React environment. jQuery, for instance, will not play nice with React, as its primary function is to interact with and manipulate the browser's native DOM. But I've even seen some strange CSS race conditions. Here are some of my recommendations for nice animations in a React workflow.

React-Motion

React-Motion (*http://bit.ly/2lSUy2l*) by Cheng Lou is considered to be the best way to animate in React, and the community has pretty much adopted it over the old `Reac tCSSTransitionGroup` (*http://bit.ly/2lkVbRs*). I like React-Motion a lot, but there are some keys to working with it that will have you banging your head for a little while if you don't get them.

React-Motion is pretty similar to game-based animation (*http://bit.ly/2lQv5Jf*), where you give an element mass and physics and send it on its way, and it gets there when it gets there—you aren't specifying an amount of time like you do with CSS or any other traditional web-based sequential motion. The motion can look realistic, which can be beautiful (*http://codepen.io/sdras/full/pyedJE/*). But the hard part is that if you have two different things that have to fire at the same time and get there at the same time, it can be tough to line them up exactly.

Recently, Cheng Lou added in `onRest` (*http://bit.ly/2lQKuJh*), which allows for this kind of callback workflow. It hasn't advanced much, though, as it's counter to the original premise of the tool. It's still not easy to write a loop (without writing an infinite loop, which is bad for a whole slew of reasons). You might never come across this use case, but I did once.

Pros:

- The animation can look really beautiful and realistic, and the spring options are nice.
- The staggering effect is pretty unique—staggering is available in most JS libraries (like GSAP and Velocity) but the spring is based directly off of the last element's movement, not *duplicating* the last one, so there are some nice motion possibilities.
- This is probably the animation tool that plays with React the best.

Cons:

- It's not super plug-and-play like some other libraries or native, which means you end up writing quite a bit more code. Some people like this about it; some people don't. It's not kind to beginners, though.
- Because of the complex nature of the code, the sequencing is not as straightforward or legible as with some of the alternatives.
- `onRest` still doesn't work for staggering parameters.

GSAP in React

GreenSock has so much to offer that it's still worth using in a React environment. It takes a bit more finessing than usual, and some things that should work (and do with the DOM) don't in React. That said, I've gotten it working a few different ways:

- Hook into the native React component lifecycle methods (*http://bit.ly/2mf3hih*).
- Hook it up to something you call for interaction. For interaction, I create a function, and then hook it into an event like `onClick`.
- There's a nice post (*http://bit.ly/2lQD7Bz*) by Chang Wang about how to hook it into `ReactTransitionGroup`, which is a pretty cool way of doing it.

- You can use a library like React-Gsap-Enhancer (*http://bit.ly/2l8hTA9*). React-Gsap-Enhancer seems like a good tool for when you're doing very complicated sequencing. For something very simple, it's probably overkill, and you could just use GSAP straight out with lifecycle methods.

Canvas in React

Canvas itself works beautifully in React. You can choose to bypass the DOM entirely and attach a single node, in which you can create all of your animations. It has the same benefits and limitations we discussed previously (see "Canvas" on page 79). You can also break a canvas into React components, but the implementation details can get much more complicated due to the virtual DOM.

There are a couple of good libraries for working with canvas in React. React-Canvas was developed by the Flipboard team because they wanted 60 fps animation with the DOM. The repo hasn't been updated in a while, though, and it really does focus on only UI elements, so any other kind of animation will take some work.

React Konva (*https://github.com/lavrton/react-konva*) is an interesting, very declarative way of working with canvas and React. It creates beautiful shapes incredibly easily, but the animation performance is a little lacking. The developer acknowledges this right in the docs, so it's possible that if you're willing to submit a pull request (PR) you could improve it and help him work on it.

CSS in React

CSS has had a resurgence lately because it's likely the easiest way to create animations in React. I like working with CSS animations for little things like UI/UX interactions, but have seen them behave a little strangely if you try to chain things using delays. Other than that, they're pretty great, especially for small UI adjustments.

Covering Ground

Unfortunately, it would be impossible to go into all of these wonderful tools in great depth—this book would be 10 times as long! We'll focus primarily on the GreenSock Animation API, due to its power and multitude of uses. We'll also cover mo.js, React-Motion, and `requestAnimationFrame()` so you know how to work with JavaScript at a bare-metal level.

CHAPTER 8

Animating with GreenSock

In the previous chapter, we went over some of the reasons you might choose Green-Sock as an animation library. In this chapter, we'll cover the basics of how to animate.

Even if you're more comfortable with CSS, you can still master GreenSock. You don't necessarily need to know everything about JavaScript to use it for animation. Certainly people who are comfortable with JavaScript will pick it up a little faster and be able to debug with a little more ease, but I do think the syntax is simple and straightforward enough that a CSS developer will be able to get to grips with it. Heck! It's even easier than CSS in some ways: CSS separates concerns by putting the keyframes in one area and applying them on the properties separately, while GreenSock allows you to manipulate everything in one spot.

GreenSock has been under development for 10 years: it was previously a Flash tool. This gives it an enormous leg up on the competition, as the designers are intimately familiar with the issues users run into. They are also very approachable, and there are some regulars around to help on the forums, so if you get stuck there's a pretty good community around to help you get back on your feet.

Let's get started!

Up and Running with GreenSock

In order to use GreenSock, you need to include TweenMax in your page by including this line of code at the base of your document: `<script src="https://cdnjs.cloud flare.com/ajax/libs/gsap/1.19.0/TweenMax.min.js"></script>`.

Replace the `/1.19.0/` with whatever the most recent version of the library is; you can find that at *https://cdnjs.com/*.

Or you can use yarn or npm in your terminal:

```
npm install gsap

yarn install gsap
```

Basic GreenSock Syntax

We'll start with a really simple example, the result of which is shown in Figure 8-1:

```
TweenMax.to(".element", 2, { x: 100 });
```

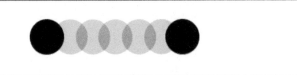

Figure 8-1. If we have a ball with a class of .element, here's what we'll see

In this example, the ball moves to the right by 100 px. Let's break down some of this syntax bit by bit, and consider a few extra options.

TweenMax/TweenLite

```
TweenMax.to(".element", 2, { x: 100 });
```

The TweenMax at the start of the statement tells the browser we're going to use the GreenSock Animation API code that was loaded from the library we imported. This can be interchanged with TweenLite, if you choose to use the smaller version of the library. The advantage of TweenLite is that it's very small, while the advantage of TweenMax is that it comes equipped with things like loops, CSS properties (which you will find you might need), and the TimelineMax library, which extends the smaller TimelineLite (we'll dig into the timeline in the next chapter). The two are interchangeable and don't change the way the animation works, aside from one having broader offerings.

.to/.from/.fromTo

```
TweenMax.to(".element", 2, { x: 100 });
```

The next piece is the .to method, which, as you might expect, tells the element to change to a different state.

You can also use .from, which means the element originates from whatever you specify in the curly braces (the animation object) and changes to its default values, or .fromTo, which gives you more granular control over where something starts and where it ends.

.fromTo becomes very useful for animations that will be retriggered, because you can be more certain of the starting and ending points. For example, say you fire an animation and it scales up by 50%. Then you ask it again to scale up by 50%—but it's already there. That animation will look like it does nothing on the secondary trigger.

When we use .fromTo, the syntax looks a little bit different:

```
TweenMax.fromTo(".element", 2, {
  x: 0
}, {
  x: 100
});
```

You can see I also broke things out over a few more lines so it's a little more legible. Now we can see fairly clearly that the element will go from the 0 coordinate on the x-axis to 100.

Staggering

We can also use .staggerTo, .staggerFrom, or .staggerFromTo. These will take the same animation and repeat it in a kind of cascade, applied to a group of objects that you designate. With SVG I find it helpful to place the items in a group together and add a class to the group to achieve this. For example, in this code, the animation will be applied to all circles inside the group with the class .element:

```
TweenMax.staggerTo(".element circle", 2, {
  x: 100
}, 0.1);
```

This code snippet shows what we've changed: we're using .staggerTo instead of .to and have added an extra parameter at the end of the statement: 0.1. *This controls the time between each of the staggers.* We're also now targeting all of the circles in a group with a class of .element. The output will look something like Figure 8-2.

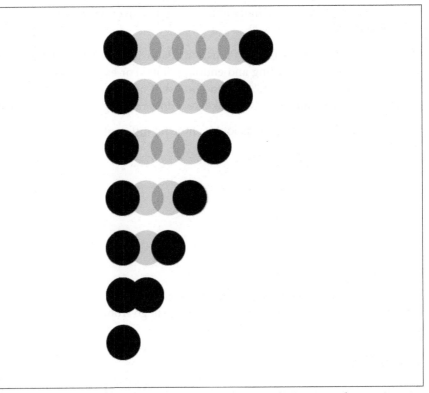

Figure 8-2. The balls are all animating with the same values, but staggered in timing, one after another

Reverse-Order Staggers

If you'd like the stagger to start from the last element and go to the first, it's very easy to do. Simply use a negative value for the interval (shown here as the `-0.1` value):

```
TweenMax.staggerTo(".element
    circle", 2, {
    x: 100
}, -0.1);
```

There are more advanced types of staggers available, including using the `cycle` property and randomized staggering values. For more information about these, check out Chapter 11.

Elements

```
TweenMax.to(".element", 2, { x: 100 });
```

The way that GreenSock targets elements is similar to `querySelector()` or `querySelectorAll()` in native JavaScript and even closer to the behavior of a jQuery selector, in that you can pass in one or multiple elements, and they can be classes, IDs, or attributes like `path`, `circle`, or `rect`. You don't have to worry about nodelists; all of that is abstracted away for you, which makes working with the DOM and cross-browser support much simpler.

You can use a quoted selector string, like in this example, to target elements directly, but GreenSock will happily accept variables too, if that's your jam (for example, `var el = document.querySelector(".el");`). I tend to use variables like this when I am targeting an element multiple times, to avoid repetition and multiple lookups.

Duration

```
TweenMax.to(.element", 2, { x: 100, delay:
    2 });
```

This is probably the simplest of the values we'll cover. We're going to pass in an integer, and it affects how long the animation will run. `2` is 2 seconds; `0.3` would be 0.3 seconds, or 300 milliseconds. Just like with the `.element` value, we can pass in a variable here too. I tend to only do that if there are multiple elements and animations that I want firing for the same exact duration, though, and that situation is fairly rare.

Delay

```
TweenMax.to(.element", 2, { x: 100, delay:
    2 });
```

If you would like to make your animation wait for a bit before firing, you can use `delay`. Delay is useful for chaining, or setting things a bit before or after one another, but in the next chapter we will cover a much more efficient and organized way to chain effects with the timeline tool.

Properties to Animate

We talked briefly about how our example code will move the ball to the right by 100 px, but let's dig into that a little more. What does that x stand for? It actually stands for `transform: translateX(100px)`. (It should *not* be confused with the x attribute in elements like `rects` in SVG.) Remember when I mentioned that transforms and opacity are the most performant things to animate? Well, GreenSock's developers know this, so they nicely created some shorthand for us—we can use `x`, `y`, `z`, `scale`, and `rotation` (instead of `rotate` in CSS). Handily, because they've broken out the properties, we can use them individually and at different times. That saves us a lot of typing and makes our code much easier to read.

Keep in mind that if you're transforming within the SVG DOM, it will use the coordinate system within the `viewBox`, so you won't actually be using true pixels. You might recall from previous chapters that this is actually a really great feature, because it means we can easily scale and create complex responsive animations (more on this in Chapter 16).

 Animating Transforms in CSS Equivalent

Because `transform` is one property in CSS, it's a hassle to apply different transforms at different times to one element. They end up having a stacking order and are applied one by one, unless you write out each value at the interpolated percentage for each change.

I've written more about this in an article for CSS-Tricks (*http:// bit.ly/2ivvcrP*).

GreenSock gives us a huge life upgrade by breaking these properties apart so we can have finer control of movement.

The CSS Working Group is planning to break transforms out into their own properties, but at the time of publishing the timeline for implementation and extent of browser support were unclear. Chrome has some experimental implementations.

We also have `opacity`, which works like it does in CSS: we can supply values from `0` to `1`, with `0` being completely transparent and `1` being completely opaque. Additionally, GreenSock offers a custom value called `autoAlpha`, which also takes values from `0` to `1`. This value couples `opacity` and `visibility: hidden`, so it removes the element from/adds it into the DOM completely.

This is important because an element with `opacity: 0` is still able to react to mouse/ touch/keyboard events and is included in the accessibility tree used by screen readers. An element with `visibility: hidden` is not. `autoAlpha` ensures that when the element has fully faded out, it is correctly hidden from interaction as well as from view.

You can also animate any number of other CSS values. Color, width, height, perspective—they're all fair game. There are a few things to keep in mind, though. First, any property with a dash in its name becomes camelCased. For example, `background-color` would be `backgroundColor`, and `border-radius` would be `borderRadius`.

Also, any value that isn't a number has to be passed in as a string, surrounded in quotes. So, a color value would be `color: "#333333"`.

When animating two properties, we separate them by commas (we treat the properties that we're animating like objects):

```
TweenMax.to(.element", 2, {
  x: 100,
  y: 50
});
```

Easing

Easing is optional, so I didn't include it in the first example. But easing is perhaps the most powerful tool in GreenSock: it brings pieces of static code to life. We can add easing as follows:

```
TweenMax.to(.element", 2, {
  x: 100,
  y: 50,
  ease: Sine.easeOut
});
```

When we write this, `ease:` always stays consistent. Here, `Sine` is the type of ease. Most of the easing curve types have three options: `.easeIn`, `.easeOut`, and `.easeInOut`. They affect which direction the Bézier shape of the ease flows in. There are many different types of GreenSock eases. When I was first learning, I found the GreenSock Ease Visualizer (*http://greensock.com/ease-visualizer*) to be an invaluable tool in visualizing and exploring all of the different options (see Figure 8-3).

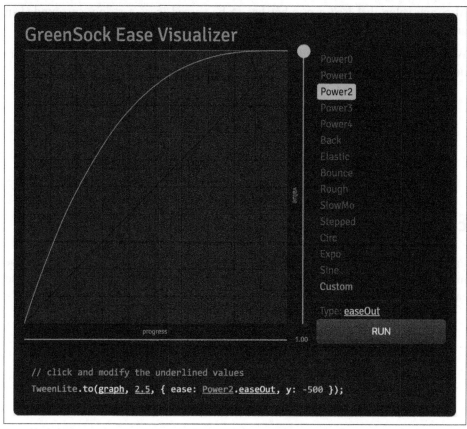

Figure 8-3. The GreenSock Ease Visualizer: an invaluable interactive tool

Recently, GreenSock introduced a new type of ease called Custom. You need to load the CustomEase plug-in in order to use it, but it enables you to pass in SVG paths, and you can play with the Ease Visualizer to manipulate the paths (which is especially nice because you can watch the demo move). This is an incredible feature, as sometimes the type of easing you use makes all the difference between awkwardness and realistic, impressive movement.

Hot Easing Tip

Despite what their names might suggest, `.easeOut` is actually really good for entrances. `.easeIn` is great for exits, and I tend to use `.easeInOut` sparingly, often for intermediary states.

In and *out* in easing refer to the beginning and end of the animation, and you want the "easy" (slower) part of the animation to be the part that's closer to the resting state of the object (the end for entrances, the beginning for exits), with faster motion as it moves offscreen.

This might seem like a lot to dig into and understand, but once you've worked with the syntax a few times, it's relatively easy to commit it to memory because you'll use the same general pattern again and again. I highly suggest typing out some of the code in this chapter to keep it fresh in your mind.

In future chapters, we'll dig into some really advanced and fun things, now that you have the basics down!

CHAPTER 9

GreenSock's Timeline

In the last chapter we covered some of the basic syntax for GreenSock tweening. In this chapter, we'll go over one of my favorite GreenSock features: the timeline.

A Simple Timeline

In the last chapter we talked about GreenSock's syntax, focusing on the `TweenMax` part of the statement. You might recall that I mentioned TweenMax includes Timeline-Max, GreenSock's full-featured timeline tool. Why is this such a good thing?

TimelineMax is a really powerful tool for controlling multiple animations and sequencing. In order to use it, you need to instantiate it. We do this by calling `var tl = new TimelineMax();` (you could also use `let` or `const` here , if you're using ES6, and you can call `tl` whatever you wish—`tl` tends to be the industry standard).

You could just use TweenMax for everything, but the default for TweenMax is to have everything fire at once. You would have to add delays to each animation to get them to fire one after another.

Let's say we want to animate the three shapes in Figure 9-1 in a row from left to right, one after another.

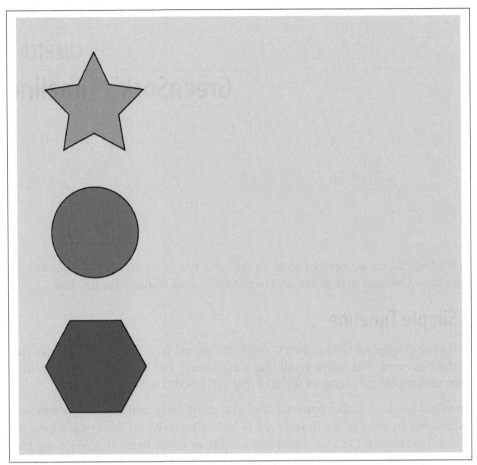

Figure 9-1. Animating in a row

So far, we've learned to express it like this:

```
TweenMax.to(".star", 3, {x: 300, ease: Power4.easeOut});
TweenMax.to(".circle", 3, {x: 300, delay:3, ease: Power4.easeOut});
TweenMax.to(".hex", 3, {x: 300, delay:6, ease: Power4.easeOut});
```

This works, but if we had more elements, we'd have to keep calculating these values. It makes a lot more sense to use a timeline, which automatically cascades them one after another for us (note that we don't need the delays here):

```
var tl = new TimelineMax();

tl.to(".star", 3, {x: 300, ease: Power4.easeOut});
tl.to(".circle", 3, {x: 300, ease: Power4.easeOut});
tl.to(".hex", 3, {x: 300, ease: Power4.easeOut});
```

This is really great, because we can keep going all day and the timeline will automatically put our animations in order for us.

So what happens if we watch this animation and decide we want the circle to start moving just a little before the star is done? We can use the position parameter that we previously saw in `.staggerTo` animations (see "Staggering" on page 89), through *relative incrementation*:

```
var tl = new TimelineMax();

tl.to(".star", 3, {x: 300, ease: Power4.easeOut});
tl.to(".circle", 3, {x: 300, ease: Power4.easeOut}, "-=1");
tl.to(".hex", 3, {x: 300, ease: Power4.easeOut});
```

Incrementing in Time

In the preceding example, we used a relative incrementor, `"-=1"`, to let the timeline know we wanted to push the animation up by one second. If you're not familiar with JavaScript, incrementors are really useful. The syntax is +=1 (or any integer) or -=1. This lets the compiler know we are taking the original state and adding to it, not setting a static value. You can see this expressed in a number of ways to work with the timeline.

For instance, we can add a delay to the timeline:

```
tl.to(".circle", 3, {x: 300}, "+=1");
```

We can set it to fire a second before it normally would (but only if the timeline already has time on it):

```
tl.to(".circle", 3, {x: 300}, "-=1");
```

Or we can set it to fire at a specific time that's static. This will fire exactly 2 seconds in:

```
tl.to(".circle", 3, {x: 300}, "2");
```

My favorite, though, is setting animations on or relative to labels, which we'll cover next.

The cool thing about this is that the circle will now start animating one second before the star finishes, but the hex will still follow the circle, even though we've adjusted the placement in time (originally the hex would have fired at six seconds; now the hex will fire at five).

Relative Labels

This is all well and good, but what if you have a *very* complex animation, and you want multiple things firing at once, far into your timeline? Or you want a few things to fire slightly before or after one another? That kind of logic can get a little tangled and disorganized, particularly if you have to adjust the timeline (which, trust me, you will need to do all the time).

Enter relative labels. Relative labels are incredibly useful, because you can insert them partway into a timeline, or you can set them at the beginning and have everything fire off of them.

Figure 9-2 is an example.

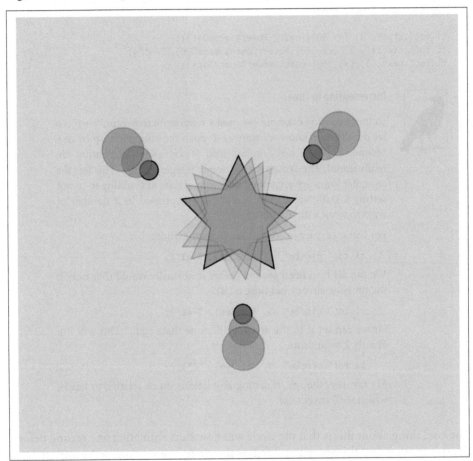

Figure 9-2. An animation where the star rotates and three circles fire at once

In this example, let's say you want the star to rotate on itself, and then immediately when it's done you want three circles to fire at the same time.

Since the circles are all animated a different way, we can't just apply the same animation to all of them (yes, we could build a function for it, but I'll address that later in the chapter). This is when a relative label will come in really handy. Rather than writing this:

```
var tl = new TimelineMax();

tl.to(".star", 3, {
  rotation: 30,
  transformOrigin: "50% 50%"
});

tl.to(".circle1", 1, {
  scale: 2.5
  x: 100,
  y: -70
});

tl.to(".circle2", 1, {
  scale: 2.5
  y: -100
}, "-=1");

tl.to(".circle3", 1, {
  scale: 2.5
  y: -70,
  x: -100
}, "-=2");
```

we can use a label:

```
var tl = new TimelineMax();

tl.to(".star", 3, {
  rotation: 30,
  transformOrigin: "50% 50%"
});

tl.add("burst");

tl.to(".circle1", 1, {
  scale: 2.5
  x: 100,
  y: -70
}, "burst");

tl.to(".circle2", 1, {
  scale: 2.5
  y: -100
}, "burst");

tl.to(".circle3", 1, {
  scale: 2.5
  y: -70,
```

```
    x: -100
  }, "burst");
```

I prefer this way because it's so much more legible to someone reading it later. It's also more flexible: anything can move earlier in the timeline, and the circles will all still burst together. Their timing can also change, and there's nothing to be recalculated. You can even set them a little before or after one another with the relative positioning we discussed earlier: `"burst+=1"`.

.set to Stabilize Your Animation

You may have times when you realize that you want to animate something like the perspective, where you actually animate the z value, but you have to set the perspective in order to see the effects. You may also want to set a stroke on a shape that doesn't have one in order to animate it with DrawSVG (*https://greensock.com/drawSVG*). You can definitely set these properties in CSS, but the nice thing about .set is that you are telling the person who is reading your code what you're changing in order to animate. It's harder to do this with the CSS in a completely different place, so this is a real maintenance boon. Basically, you are "setting" the tween without animating it:

```
    tl.set(".circle", {scale: 0.5});
```

You might not always need a set, though—if you have a `.fromTo` animation that designates a different state for the element to originate from, it will carry through the whole animation. So if you decided to do something like:

```
    tl.fromTo(".circle", {
      scale: 0.5
    }, {
      scale: 1
    }, 8);
```

even if it's 8 seconds into the animation, the `"from"` state will be applied to the whole length of the animation before it.

That said, another good use of `.set` is for things you animate with a `.from` or `.fromTo`. For instance, if you have something with `opacity: 0` at the outset, you'll notice that there's a momentary flash on the screen of the element shown while the JavaScript is loading. It's usually only for a split second, but discernible to the naked eye.

Since the CSS is loaded first, a workaround would be to set the visibility to `hidden` in the CSS:

```
    .element { visibility: hidden; }
```

and then set it back to `visible` in the JavaScript, so that GSAP can handle it from there:

```
TweenMax.set(".element", {visibility:"visible"});
```
I use this trick in almost every pen or project that I make.

Nested and Master Timelines

I don't suggest just throwing some animations into your global scope. If you're working with a really simple TweenMax animation, it's easy enough to pack your animation into an IIFE (immediately invoked function expression), but I strongly suggest
wrapping your timelines in a function and calling that instead.

One step further would be to create a master timeline. I like using master timelines
because I can group sections of the animation into scenes. This gives me tons of control because I can:

- Name and order my scenes so that it's easy to find my place when I have to make
  adjustments.
- Change the placement of these scenes.
- Make just one scene a little faster.
- Seek out a scene so that I don't have to sit through the entire animation every
  time.
- Restart or play the master timeline on an event, like a click.
- Keep all of my animations organized, tidy, and easy to read.

Let's dig into how to create a master timeline, and then we'll go through all the bells
and whistles.

Organization

Here is an example of how I set up a timeline and apply it to a master:

```
function sceneOne() {
  var tl = new TimelineMax();

  tl.add("begin");
  tl.to(".bubble", 2, {
      scale: 3,
      opacity: 0.5,
      rotation: 90,
      ease: Circ.easeOut
  }, "begin");
  ...

  return tl;
}

var master = new TimelineMax();
master.add(sceneOne(), "scene1");
```

In this example, we've placed the timeline in a function (you don't need to call it sce neOne()—you can name it whatever you wish). At the end of the function, we return the timeline. We then add the scene function to a master timeline. You may notice that I used a position label for the scene as well. I do this so that I may quickly reference it while I'm working. (I'll show what I mean by that in a second.)

Now, if we want to add more scenes, it's really easy:

```
function sceneOne() {
  var tl = new TimelineMax();

  tl.add("begin");
  tl.to(".bubble", 2, {
      scale: 3,
      opacity: 0.5,
      rotation: 90,
      ease: Circ.easeOut
  }, "begin");
  ...

  return tl;
}

function sceneTwo() {
  var tl = new TimelineMax();

  tl.add("boom");
  tl.to(".star", 2, {
      scale: 5,
      opacity: 0,
      rotation: -360,
      ease: Circ.easeIn
  }, "boom");
  ...

  return tl;
}

var master = new TimelineMax();
master.add(sceneOne(), "scene1")
      .add(sceneTwo(), "scene2");
```

We can even easily change their order around if we want:

```
var master = new TimelineMax();
master.add(sceneTwo(), "scene2")
      .add(sceneOne(), "scene1");
```

.seek for a Better Workflow

Eventually, your animations might start getting really long. It becomes hard to adjust a single part and keep in your mind what you're changing if you have to watch everything that came before it. For this, .seek is a huge boon to your workflow. This is where the position labels come in really handy. Sometimes when I watch a full animation, even if it's only seconds long, I forget exactly what I was adjusting. This way, I can go directly into scene2, three seconds in, and watch only the one part I'm adjusting:

```
var master = new TimelineMax();
master.add(sceneOne(), "scene1")
      .add(sceneTwo(), "scene2");

master.seek("scene2+=3");
```

Fairly often, I'll finish a really long animation and notice one scene is just a little too fast or too slow. For this, I take advantage of the timeScale() method. This is a pretty powerful GreenSock feature, and you'd be surprised how often it comes in handy. I've even had animations where I split up the functions in a different organization so that I could use timeScale() to refine them. Here's an example:

```
function sceneOne() {
  var tl = new TimelineMax();

  tl.add("begin");
  tl.to(".bubble", 2, {
      scale: 3,
      opacity: 0.5,
      rotation: 90,
      ease: Circ.easeOut
  }, "begin");
  ...

  tl.timeScale(1.5);

  return tl;
}
```

This will make all of the animations in scene1 1.5 times faster. For slower animation, we would change the scale to be less than 1: i.e., 0.5 would be slower by half.

Loops

If we wanted to repeat an animation, we would say repeat: -1, but what about if we wanted to repeat an entire section? We would add that object in as a parameter to that timeline. Here's an example:

```
function sceneOne() {
  var tl = new TimelineMax({ repeat: -1 });

  tl.add("begin");
  tl.to(".bubble", 2, {
      scale: 3,
      opacity: 0.5,
      rotation: 90,
      ease: Circ.easeOut
  }, "begin");
  ...

  return tl;
}
```

We can also use yoyos (the syntax is a Boolean value, yoyo:true) if we want the animation to oscillate between playing backward and forward. This can be applied to individual tweens, full timelines, or master timelines, but yoyos will only work if the timeline is repeated. If we wanted to apply this kind of logic to the whole master timeline, we would add it the same way, into the master's timeline call:

```
var master = new TimelineMax({repeat: -1, yoyo:true});
```

When we repeat things, we also have the benefit of applying a specific delay to the whole thing. delay: 1 would delay all of the animation without a pause in between repetitons of the animation, while repeatDelay: 1 would pause the animation in between each iteration.

Repeat Usage

The rest of the methods described here are available to both TimelineLite and TimelineMax, but looping, repeats, and yoyos are exclusive to TimelineMax.

Please also be aware that if an animation is looped or retriggered, you might consider using .fromTo instead of .to to make sure that it starts from exactly where you need it to instead of where it left off.

You don't have to repeat things this way; you can also use callbacks if they make more sense to you or if you're changing things (like making something random) on every loop. Callbacks also have a lot of power if you need to make things more precise. The syntax looks like this:

```
function _flyBy(el, amt) {
  TweenMax.to(el, amt, {
    x: -200,
    rotation: 360,
    onComplete: this._flyBy,
    onCompleteParams: [el, amt]
```

```
    });
  }
```

If we were to use this type of callback to create a random effect, we'd do something like this:

```
function _flyBy(el) {
    TweenMax.to(el, amt, {
      x: Math.random() * 400 - 200,
      rotation: Math.random() * 360,
      onComplete: _flyBy,
      onCompleteParams: [el]
    });
  }
```

The onComplete option gives the name of the callback function (to be called when the animation has completed), and the onCompleteParams option lets us declare an array of parameters that GreenSock will use when it calls that function. In this code, we told it to call the function _flyBy with the values stored in the el and amt variables. This is useful because normally, if you just repeat a random number, the compiler reads it once, and then it's not really "random."

There are many ways to work with callbacks, including defining the *scope* (changing what this refers to in the function) and deciding when they are called. The available options include:

- onStart
- onStartScope
- onStartParams
- onComplete
- onCompleteScope
- onCompleteParams
- onUpdate
- onUpdateScope
- onUpdateParams
- onRepeat
- onRepeatScope
- onRepeatParams
- onReverseComplete
- onReverseCompleteScope

callbackScope is a simple way of setting all of these at once: onStartScope, onUpdateScope, onCompleteScope, onReverseCompleteScope, and onRepeatScope.

Pausing and Events

You may recall earlier when we restarted the whole timeline by passing `repeat: -1` as an object to the `TimelineMax()` constructor. Similarly, you can set a whole timeline to be paused initially:

```
var master = new TimelineMax({paused: true});
```

This is especially useful if you want a timeline to be paused when the page is first visited, and the animation activated with a click:

```
var master = new TimelineMax({paused: true});
...

var el = document.getElementById("button")
el.addEventListener('click', function(e) {
  e.preventDefault();
  master.restart();
}, false);
```

Pretty simple!

We can, of course, use all sorts of events here. With tools like Hammer.js (*http://hammerjs.github.io/*), you can have touch events on mobile retrigger timelines so that you can achieve beautiful animation effects just like you see in native apps—on swipe, on double-tap, and so on.

In Chapter 12, I'll show you how to use GreenSock's Draggable to control a timeline on drag. We could also hook a timeline up to jQuery's slider UI to make a nice scrubbing interface. Chris Gannon's ScrubGSAPTimeline (*http://bit.ly/2lYp1P4*) tool is awesome for timeline workflows. There's more information about how to use it in a pen (*http://bit.ly/2mB4pKv*).

Other Timeline Methods

GreenSock's timeline tool has too many features to cover in just one section; what follows is just a selection of what's available to you. We've gone over what I consider the most vital basics, but if any other methods are interesting to you, head over to the GreenSock docs (*https://greensock.com/docs/#/HTML5/*) or forums (*https://greensock.com/forums/*) for more information. Most of the methods are named pretty intuitively, but the docs can help clarify usage.

Keep in mind that there's an ActionScript version of GSAP too, so be mindful that you're in the JavaScript section. It's pretty easy to tell which is which, because the look/feel of the ActionScript section is much older and it has a grey design instead of their usual black and green.

TimelineLite and TimelineMax methods

- add()
- addLabel()
- addPause()
- call()
- clear()
- delay()
- duration()
- eventCallback
- exportRoot()
- from()
- fromTo()
- getChildren()
- getLabelTime()
- getTweensOf()
- invalidate()
- isActive()
- kill()
- pause()
- paused()
- play()
- progress()
- remove()
- removeLabel()
- render()
- restart()
- resume()
- reverse()
- reversed()
- seek()
- set()
- shiftChildren()
- staggerFrom()
- staggerFromTo()
- staggerTo()
- startTime()
- time()
- timeScale()
- to()
- totalDuration()

- totalProgress()
- totalTime()
- useFrames()

Methods exclusive to TimelineMax

- currentLabel()
- getActive()
- getLabelAfter()
- getLabelBefore()
- getlLabelsArray()
- repeat()
- repeatDelay()
- tweenFromTo()
- tweenTo()
- yoyo()

Now that you're all set up with the basics of the GreenSock timeline and all the power it offers, let's move on to the really fancy and fun animation extras available to you.

CHAPTER 10

MorphSVG and Motion Along a Path

There are a lot of amazing features available as plug-ins for GreenSock. The first ones we'll go over are MorphSVG and motion along a path (BezierPlugin), because these two features are virtual powerhouses for realistic movement in SVG.

Loading Plug-ins

MorphSVG is a paid-for plug-in, but chances are you'll want to play with it before you spend money. GreenSock makes this possible by providing CodePen-safe versions of its plug-ins (*http://bit.ly/ 2lv1xhg*), which you can use in pens as you like.

Don't forget to load the plug-in resources and *TweenMax.min.js* into your pen before you get started!

MorphSVG

One of the most exciting features of GreenSock is MorphSVG. At the time of publishing, GreenSock is the only library that supports tweening paths using an unequal number of path points. SnapSVG, SMIL, and even D3 allow you to change a path's shape into another one, but if the path points are uneven, the morph either fails or looks incredibly ugly and unwieldy. MorphSVG can mutate shapes with uneven path points beautifully, and with `findShapeIndex()` you can even fine-tune the type of morph that's created.

In order to morph an SVG path into another, all you need to do is point from one ID to another. *Seriously, it's just that simple.* And you can create the most amazing effects. The syntax looks like this:

```
TweenMax.to("#pathFrom", 1, {morphSVG:"#pathTo"});
```

MorphSVG will honor where the path is in the viewBox, so keep in mind when you make your SVGs that you should have the paths you are morphing from and to in the same position, or the shape will move to the other location when it starts animating.

You can also morph polyline and polygon elements, either with the preceding ID syntax or by supplying the polygon points as a string directly:

```
TweenLite.to("#polygon", 2, {morphSVG:"10,10 40,70 70,70 70,10"});
```

MorphSVG is built for paths and polygons/polylines, but you might find that sometimes you need to animate circles, rects, or other SVG elements. The plug-in offers the method convertToPath() to convert these easily. You can either call it using an ID or class associated with the target element, or pass in the full element to convert them all at once from the start:

```
MorphSVGPlugin.convertToPath("circle, rect, ellipse, line, polygon, polyline");
```

Plug-in Compatibility

MorphSVG and TweenMax are both pretty complex, and they are worked on regularly and receive regular upgrades. It's important to use compatible versions of each file because a lot of care is taken to increment the versions in tandem. I've seen student animations fail when they use the latest version of TweenMax and an older version of MorphSVG, so if you're having trouble getting a simple morph to work (and I would start with something simple first), you might want to check that you're working with compatible versions.

findShapeIndex()

Most often, MorphSVG does some really nice calculations under the hood to figure out what kind of transition will look appropriate with the interpolation of the different path points, so the default of auto for the shapeIndex property will work just fine. But every once in a while, you'll want to fine-tune the movement between the two.

The findShapeIndex() utility function plug-in helps you pick the best type of morph for your animation by letting you cycle through the tweening points, if you want to be particular about the way the shape morphs. You load it up, point it from one ID to another (e.g., findShapeIndex("#hex", "#star");), and a nice GUI appears. Don't leave this in your codebase, though—you should use it and then discard it before putting things into production so you don't add extra weight unnecessarily.

In Figure 10-1 and the corresponding demo (*http://bit.ly/2g8CCyg*), you can see how I'm tweening the star into the decagon, but the index completely changes how they interpolate. The more path points you have, the more complex your choices will be. Fewer path points provide fewer options.

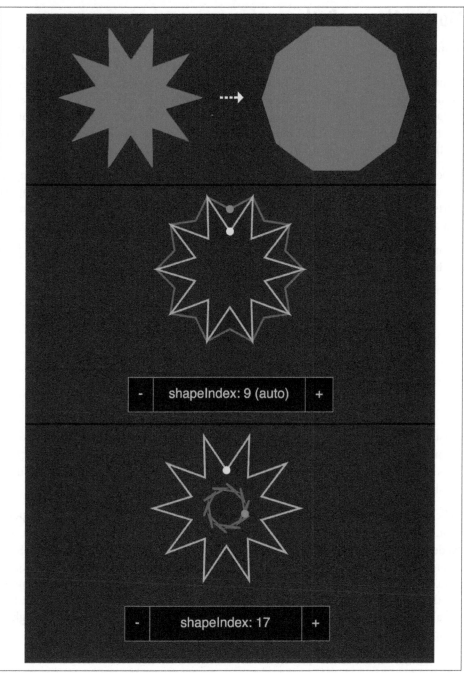

Figure 10-1. The two shapes we'd like to morph (top), the GUI that comes up when find-ShapeIndex() is loaded and shapeIndex is set to auto (middle), and a different shape morph when we adjust the index to another integer

Motion Along a Path

Motion along a path is truly vital for realistic movement in animation. Interpolating single values in the x, y, and z directions will only get you so far. Consider the movement of a firefly in a jar—living beings rarely sail along in a linear fashion. Currently, motion along a path is not supported in CSS, though it is coming down the pipeline (*http://dev.w3.org/fxtf/motion-1/*), and you can vote to support its implementation in Microsoft Edge (*http://bit.ly/2mznqf8*). SMIL offers motion along a path, but no SMIL support is offered in IE or Edge (*http://caniuse.com/#search=smil*).

GreenSock provides a stable way to create such an effect using the BezierPlugin, included in TweenMax, providing support in IE8+ (for HTML content, SVG support starts at IE9). Thus, it's currently the most fully supported and backward-compatible way to work with motion along a path.

In order to create a motion along a path, pass an array of coordinates as values into the bezier definition:

```
TweenMax.to($firefly1, 6, {
  bezier: {
    type: "soft",
    values:[{x:10, y:30}, {x:-30, y:20}, {x:-40, y:10},
            {x:30, y:20}, {x:10, y:30}],
    autoRotate: true
  },
  ease: Linear.easeNone,
  repeat: -1
}, "start+=3");
```

I usually use x and y values, which are the transform coordinates we mentioned before, but other values would work as well, such as left, top, or even rotation. This also means you can animate along 3D Bézier paths by adding a z value! Super flexible. But 99% of the time, I just use x, y.

When we use x and y, the coordinates refer to points relative to the element's position, not the canvas itself. In other words, if you specify x:5, y:10, the motion will be defined from 5 to the right and 10 down from where the element is currently. Subsequent points are still defined by the element's initial position, not the last coordinate. This makes plotting points in an area much easier to map around the element. In the case of these particular fireflies (*http://codepen.io/sdras/full/MYQxXe/*), I tweaked the path to stay within the bounds of the light bulb, and also look slightly jumpy, as in realistic movement bugs tend to hop around a bit (Figure 10-2).

Figure 10-2. Fireflies move around in a peculiar manner; to animate them realistically, they should not move in a linear fashion and they need to rotate along with the path

Let's say you aren't animating fireflies. Perhaps you'd like to use the paths as general coordinates, but want the motion between them to be smooth and refined. There are two ways of achieving this. The first is to set the type parameter to "soft". This will take the paths you feed it and curve toward these points, as if being pulled in their direction, rather than interpolating the values to one set and then the next. The other, more nuanced way that offers more control is to set type to thru (this is the default) and define a curviness value. 0 defines no curviness, 1 is normal, 2 is twice as curvy, and so on. Figure 10-3 and its corresponding pen example (*http://codepen.io/sdras/ full/PqEPqz*) show the effects of this setting.

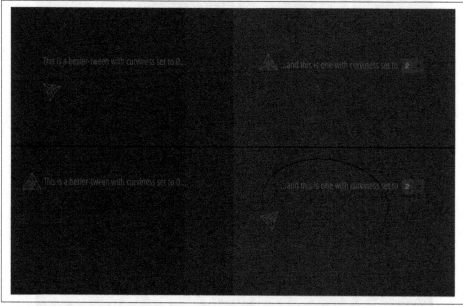

Figure 10-3. Demo showing the curve of the motion set to different curviness parameters

Note that past a value of 3 the curve begins to look less smooth overall, because each point is beginning to loop around its own axis. You can think of the motion as being a little like twanging a rubber band: when we set curviness to 0, the rubber band is pulled taut. When we set it to 2, the rubber band is a little loose—just enough for the motion to look smooth between points. When we get to 8 or so, the motion begins to unravel.

In addition to "thru" and "soft", we have two other specifications for Bézier types: "quadratic" and "cubic". "quadratic" allows you to define a control point between each anchor. "cubic" is similar, but you can specify two control points between each anchor. For both "quadratic" and "cubic", you must begin and end the array with an anchor, though you can use as many iterations as you like.

For now, you pass an array of coordinates, though I wouldn't be surprised if in the future GSAP added the ability to use an SVG path itself as the definition for the movement. This library constantly adds new features; you can watch the repository (*https://github.com/greensock/GreenSock-JS/*) for updates and see what's been added in the past year.

We also mentioned rotation. In the earlier pen, I simply used `autoRotate: true` to have each firefly spin on its own axis that correlates to the direction of the line while it travels through the array. You can be more specific by setting `autoRotate` to an integer rather than a Boolean, to set the initial degree of the element before it begins spinning. You may also pass an array, to adjust these options:

1. Position property 1 (typically `"x"`)
2. Position property 2 (typically `"y"`)
3. Rotational property (typically `"rotation"`, but can also be `"rotationX"` or `"rotationY"` if you'd like it to stay on one axis)
4. (Optional) Number of degrees (or radians) to add to the new rotation at the onset
5. Boolean value indicating whether the rotational property should be defined in radians rather than degrees (the default is `false`, which results in degrees)

Setting the array to `autoRotate: ["x","y","rotation",0,false]` is the same thing as using `autoRotate:true`, and the element will follow the rotation trajectory of the path it's following. The parameter I use the most often of these five is number 4: the number of degrees to add to the new rotation. This helps tilt the character or element in a certain direction at the outset of the animation. This is really helpful because realistic motion usually calls for tweaking the direction of rotation at the outset—things don't usually just move directly forward or start in a stable horizontal direction.

I've provided a toggle for `autoRotate: true` and `false` in Figures 10-4 and 10-5 and their corresponding example (*http://codepen.io/sdras/full/aOZOwj/*), so that you can see precisely the effect this parameter has on the animation.

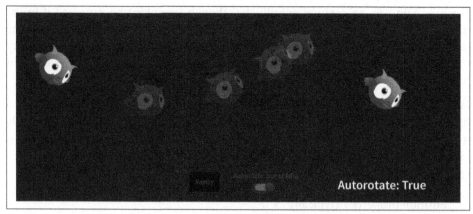

Figure 10-4. When autorotate: true is used, the element/character tilts to follow the path

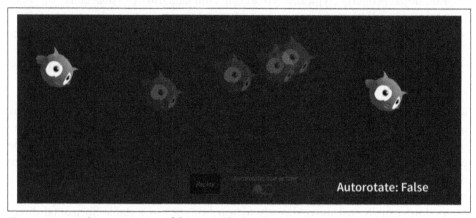

Figure 10-5. When autorotate: false is used, the element/character doesn't follow the path, and the motion feels a little awkward

Here's the code:

```
function lilGuyGo(autoRotate) {
  // bring playhead back to beginning and clear all tweens
  tl.progress(0).clear()
  // set the initial rotation to be close to the direction he's headed in
  .set(lilG, {
    rotation: 40
  });
  // tween added to timeline with the specified Bezier paths
  tl.to(lilG, 3, {
    bezier: {
      type: "soft",
      values: [{x: 0, y: 50}, {x: 150, y: 100}, {x: 300, y: 50},
               {x: 500, y: 200}, {x: 700, y: 100}, {x: 900, y: 80}],
      autoRotate: "true"
```

```
    },
    // ease for slip-n-slide-like animation-wheeee!
    ease: Circ.easeInOut
  });
}
lilGuyGo(true);
```

The little character looks much more alive this way than if he had statically been set to any degree angle during the course of the tween. You can also see that I set his initial rotation to face down toward the direction he'd be autorotating to—that's because if I hadn't, there would have been a little "jump" as he tried to right himself along the correct origin and axis. I could have also passed that in as an option in autoRotate, as specified previously. Either way works.

Motion along a path does not just apply to character animation, of course. When paired with other types of opacity and transform animations, there are endless possibilities for expressive yet fine-tuned control over animations.

CHAPTER 11

Stagger Effects, Tweening HSL, and SplitText for Text Animation

Staggered Animations

The stagger feature in a lot of JavaScript animation libraries tends to be an incredibly useful tool for creating elegant animations, which is definitely a benefit over using a CSS workflow to create the same effect. Let's take a look at a few different ways (*http://bit.ly/2fPAV8d*) to write the staggering animation illustrated in Figure 11-1.

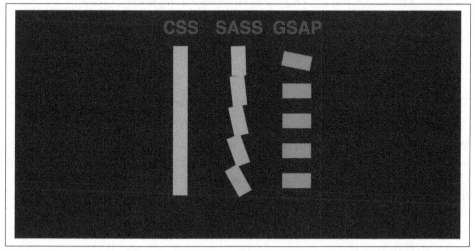

Figure 11-1. Comparing writing the same staggering animation in CSS, Sass, and GSAP

To create a stagger effect in CSS, you increment the delay using the element or pseudoelement with the same keyframes:

```
@keyframes staggerFoo {
  to {
    background: orange;
    transform: rotate(90deg);
  }
}

.css .bar:nth-child(1) { animation: staggerFoo 1s 0.1s ease-out both; }
.css .bar:nth-child(2) { animation: staggerFoo 1s 0.2s ease-out both; }
.css .bar:nth-child(3) { animation: staggerFoo 1s 0.3s ease-out both; }
.css .bar:nth-child(4) { animation: staggerFoo 1s 0.4s ease-out both; }
.css .bar:nth-child(5) { animation: staggerFoo 1s 0.5s ease-out both; }
.css .bar:nth-child(6) { animation: staggerFoo 1s 0.5s ease-out both; }
```

In Sass, you could DRY it out a little:

```
@keyframes staggerFoo {
  to {
    background: orange;
    transform: rotate(90deg);
  }
}

@for $i from 1 through 6 {
  .sass .bar:nth-child(#{$i} ) {
    animation: staggerFoo 1s ($i * 0.1s) ease-out both;
  }
}
```

However, with GSAP, you can create this effect with a single line of code:

```
TweenMax.staggerTo(".gsap .bar", 1, {
  backgroundColor: "orange",
  rotation: 90,
  ease: Sine.easeOut
}, 0.1);
```

The fact that it's so concise is good for workflow, especially if things need to be adjusted down the line.

With the use of the `cycle` property here we can pass in multiple values to stagger between, something that would take a lot of complex `nth-child` Sass operations in CSS. The syntax calls for an array of values, and it will pass the elements between those values:

```
TweenMax.staggerTo(".foo", 1, {
cycle: {
  y: [75, 0, -75]
},
ease: Power4.easeInOut
}, 0.05);
```

You can also randomize these for even more interesting effects. This works better than creating a randomizing helper function and calling it, as at runtime we'll only call the randomizing function once (and therefore it won't be random). This use of the cycle property allows us to create really beautiful and interesting effects easily. In the following code we're using the cycle property to randomly generate values for each animation:

```
var coord = [40, 800, 70, -200];

TweenMax.staggerTo(".foo", 1, {
  cycle: {
    x: function(i) {
      return coord[Math.floor(Math.random() * coord.length)];
    }
  },
  ease: Power4.easeInOut
}, 0.1);
```

 ### Understanding Math.random() for Animation

Math.random() is incredibly useful for animating in JavaScript due to its ability to create mesmerizing random effects or spin up generative code. Math.random() returns a number between 0 and 1, so you can see how it would be useful out of the box for things like opacity, where that range directly applies. In other cases, you multiply it by the maximum value you want, creating a range from 0 to that value. In the preceding code, you might have noticed that we placed Math.random() inside the Math.floor() method. This causes the result to be rounded to the next lowest integer value (Math.ceil() would round up, and Math.round() would round to the nearest integer. Although both .floor() and .round() work in this case, I usually opt for .floor() because I've read that the performance is ever so slightly better. Of course, if you don't need to snap to integer values, it is even more performant not to round at all.

If you need Math.random() to scale in between a range that doesn't start at 0, you'll have to multiply it by the difference between the values and add the minimum value, like this:

```
Math.random() * (max - min) + min;
```

In Figure 11-2 and the corresponding example (*http://codepen.io/sdras/pen/ XmmjQb*), I simply staggered between three values for each target. With very little code (22 lines of JavaScript), you can accomplish so much!

Figure 11-2. All of this animation was possible with very little code thanks to GSAP's ability to tween an array of values across a lot of objects

Here's the code:

```
var bP = $(".boggle path"),
    tl = new TimelineLite();

tl.add("start");
tl.staggerFrom(bP, 3, {
  cycle:{
    fill:["white", "yellow", "#e23e0c"],
    opacity:[0.8, 0.2, 0.5, 0.3],
  },
  ease:Elastic.easeOut
}, 0.001);
tl.staggerTo(bP, 3, {
  cycle:{
    y:[700, -700, -1000, 1000],
    x:[200, -200, -700, 700],
    rotation: function(i) {
      return i * 20
    }
  },
  opacity: 0,
  fill: "#f2bf30",
  ease:Circ.easeInOut
}, 0.001, "start+=1.25");
```

Relative HSL Color Animation

This one is relatively simple. Get it? Relative? Hoo boy. The ability to tween relative HSL (hue, saturation, lightness) color amounts is fantastic, because if you want to create sophisticated color effects easily in animations, slightly adjusting these values yields very powerful visuals.

Say you wanted to slowly turn a whole scene, with every element a slightly different color, from day to night. Previously the easiest way to do so was to gradually change the color value of each of these elements individually. You could put an overlay on the whole container, but that lacks sophistication and realism. Or perhaps, you could use an SVG fe- matrix filter, but this is unsemantic and not very intuitive to animate. Or you might try using a CSS filter that doesn't yet have a ton of support.

With GSAP, however, with one small piece of code you can uniformly, and with great backward compatibility, grab hundreds of elements and make them slightly darker, decrease their relative saturation, and slowly adjust their hue to turn them a slightly different shade. Tweening HSL also has the benefit of being able to be used for both background (for divs) or fill (for SVG), because it's not opinionated toward a certain type of property.

Figure 11-3 and the corresponding example (*http://codepen.io/sdras/pen/zvwGKw*) show how it works.

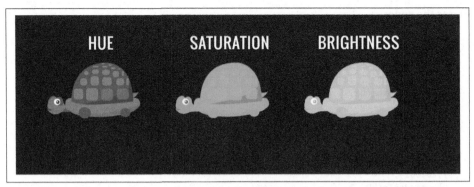

Figure 11-3. When you hover over a turtle, the fill of every shape in the turtle SVG is interpolated by a relative hue, saturation, or lightness value

So many options! What's a good use case? We can put the stagger cycle and the HSL color tweening together with some interaction. But instead of a night scene, let's make it a little more wild.

We'll make two different buttons with slightly different relative effects. Because we are tweening relative values, we can combine effects on the buttons and get multiple outputs:

```
// button hue
function hued() {

// keeps the fill and background consistent while relative hue changes
  var ch1 = "hsl(+=110, +=0%, +=0%)",
  tl = new TimelineMax({
    paused: true
  });

  tl.add("hu");

  tl.to(mult, 1.25, {
      fill: ch1
    }, "hu");

// tweens for background because of divs and CSS
  tl.to(body, 1.25, {
      backgroundColor: ch1
    }, "hu");

// the gauge responds to the action in the scene as if it's showing pressure

  tl.from(gauge, 2, {
      rotation: "-=70",
      transformOrigin: "50% 50%",
      ease: Bounce.easeOut
    }, "hu");
```

```
    return tl;
  }

  var hue = hued();
```

We'll also make the scene stagger in with a bit more nuance using the `cycle` property. But because we want all of the elements to come in and eventually look the same, it makes more sense to use `.staggerFrom` than `.staggerTo`:

```
tl.staggerFrom(city, 0.75, {
    y: -50,
    scale: 0,
    cycle:{
      x:[300, 100, 200],
      opacity:[0.5, 0.3, 0.2, 0.8],
      rotation:[50, 100, 150],
    },
    transformOrigin: "50% 50%",
    ease: Back.easeOut
  }, 0.02, "in");
```

And that becomes our city constructor set (Figure 11-4).

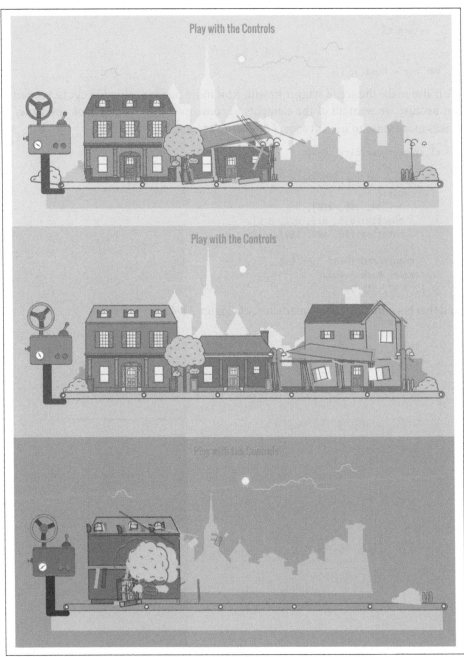

Figure 11-4. We can create controls to change all of the fill and background based on relative values, and make unique color combinations

Here, we pair relative HSL tweening with interaction and Draggable to control a timeline. Aside from some interesting effects that can be spun up very easily, Green-Sock works really well with user manipulation. We'll talk about this in Chapter 12.

SplitText

Though SplitText (*https://greensock.com/SplitText*) is not used for SVG animation, I find it useful to animate text in conjunction with SVG animation to tell a story. Although I'm covering it in this book, SplitText is not meant to work with SVG <text> nodes.

SplitText is backward compatible to IE8, and works independently of GreenSock. It works by dividing the text into characters, words, or lines, depending on which you choose, and wrapping them into individual divs so that you can manipulate them, either individually or progressively, in sequence.

Here's a simple example:

```
new SplitText("#myTextID")
```

In Figure 11-5 and its corresponding demo (*http://codepen.io/sdras/full/RNWaMX*), we're using SplitText as an object that we can use to access characters and words to animate.

Figure 11-5. Animating words can help reinforce your story

Here's the code:

```
// when you're feeling low
function sceneOne() {
  var tl = new TimelineLite(),
    mySplitText = new SplitText($text, {
      type: "chars, words"
    });

  tl.staggerFrom(mySplitText.chars, 0.8, {
      opacity: 0,
      scaleX: 0,
      ease: Power4.easeOut
    }, 0.05, "+=4")
    .staggerTo(mySplitText.words, 0.8, {
      rotationY: 60,
      y: 300,
      opacity: 0,
      ease: Power4.easeIn
    }, 0.1, "+=0.1")
    .to(person, 3, {
      rotation: -5,
      transformOrigin: "80% 50%",
      y: -10,
      ease: Circ.easeOut
    })
    .to(head, 3, {
      rotation: -10,
      transformOrigin: "0% 100%",
      y: 10,
      ease: Back.easeOut
    }, "-=3")
    .to(neck, 3, {
      rotation: -10,
      transformOrigin: "0% 100%",
      y: 10,
      ease: Back.easeOut
    }, "-=3");

  return tl;
}
```

SplitText is not the only library that can create text effects, but one killer feature I've noticed other libraries don't usually offer is that it *honors natural line breaks.*

Split elements can also have their position set as "relative" or "absolute". When you split using position: "relative", text will be able to break and wrap naturally as the parent element changes size. When using position: "absolute", text will not wrap after it is split; however, this may increase animation performance.

If you need to animate the text but then return it to its "unsplit" state, you can use the revert() method. You can also add an autoincrementing class to each broken-apart piece of text, such as .char1, .char2, .char3, etc.:

```
new SplitText("#myTextID", {type:"words", wordsClass:"char++"});
```

This allows us to create interesting effects or even target particular words, characters, or lines for specific motion.

CHAPTER 12

DrawSVG and Draggable

Draggable

Dragging objects around your screen on the web is one of those things that seems like it would be pretty easy to implement—until you try to do it from scratch. There's a lot to account for, with touch input, mouse events, viewports, scroll behavior, friction, and believable physics. There are more failure conditions than you would probably initially consider. Thankfully, GreenSock's Draggable (*https://greensock.com/draggable*) is a really powerful plug-in and works perfectly on SVG as well as HTML elements.

Draggable is device-enabled for touchscreens, uses `requestAnimationFrame()`, and is GPU-accelerated. Draggable works on its own but is more powerful when coupled with the ThrowPropsPlugin (*https://greensock.com/throwpropsplugin*), which creates really beautiful physics-like motion.

One of the best things about Draggable is its simplicity. This is all it takes to make a box realistically draggable:

```
Draggable.create(".box", {type:"x,y", edgeResistance:0.65,
  bounds:"#container", throwProps:true});
```

You may notice in the preceding code that we've defined some boundaries with bounds. bounds is pretty flexible: you can define containing units or pixel parameters. Something like `"#container"` (as in the preceding example) or `section` would work, but you could also say `{top:10, left:10, width:800, height:600}` in an object to restrict the movement.

You can also have it lock movement along the horizontal or vertical axis if you like by setting `lockAxis:true`, which will work in both directions.

There are lots of callbacks/event listeners available to you:

- `onPress`
- `onDragStart`
- `onDrag`
- `onDragEnd`
- `onRelease`
- `onLockAxis`
- `onClick`

so you can do things like:

```
myBox.addEventListener("dragend", functionName);
```

this refers to the Draggable instance itself, so you can easily access its target or bounds. That's extremely helpful, because if you are going to plug into any of Draggable's offerings, there's no guessing or console logging to figure out what you're referring to. All of this also works on transformed elements as well, and honors `transform-origin`, which is also a little hairy to write with native methods—but the plug-in makes it simple and straightforward. Figure 12-1 and its corresponding example (*http://codepen.io/sdras/pen/gbERKQ*) are demos of this plug-in.

Figure 12-1. A really simple Mr. Potato Head pen that allows you to drag pieces of an SVG around to mix and match its features

With all of the code you've learned so far, you could probably guess that the only thing we really need to make this pen fully functional is the following code:

```
var features = "#top_hat, #moustache, #redhat, #curly-moustache,
    #eyes1, #lips, #toothy-lips, #toupe, #toothy, #big-ear-r,
    #big-ear-l, #shoes1, #lashed, #lash2, #lazy-eyes, #longbrown-moustache,
    #purplehat, #sm-ear-r, #sm-ear-l, #earring-r, #earring-l, #highheels,
    #greenhat, #shoes2, #blonde, #blond-mustache, #elf-r, #elf-l";
```

```
Draggable.create(features, {
    edgeResistance:0.65,
    type:"x,y",
    throwProps:true,
    autoScroll:true
});
```

Drag Types

So far we've only shown how to use Draggable with x and y values, meaning flicking and dragging things around the screen up and down, left and right. But there are other drag types to choose from, "rotation" and "scroll":

```
Draggable.create("#wheel", {type: "rotation"});
```

Using Draggable in a rotation can be fun and engaging for controls like knobs, gears, levers, and pulleys. You can also define a minRotation and a maxRotation.

I don't tend to mess around with scrolling unless I have to, but it's important to mention that Draggable can be used for this as well. You can control the scrollTop and/or scrollLeft properties of an element; pass a Boolean value for lockAxis; and define edgeResistance, which would be a number.

One thing I do like that relates to scrolling but applies to x,y is the ability to do something like autoScroll:1 (or autoScroll:2, etc.). What this does is allow the viewport to be scrolled if the element that you're moving goes outside of the display area. Let's say you have a box dragging around a screen. If you pass in autoScroll:1, the scroll will follow the edge of the box, which is the behavior you'd expect, so it looks pretty natural.

hitTest()

One of the coolest features of Draggable is its custom collision detection. This opens up tons of possibilities for drag-and-drop UIs, interaction, and even things like games.

In the following code, we're checking if the elements are overlapping by more than 80%. If they are, we add a class (which will add a red border), and if not, we remove it:

```
var droppables = document.querySelectorAll('.box'),
    overlapThreshold = "80%";

Draggable.create(droppables, {
  bounds:window,
  onDrag: function(e) {
    var i = droppables.length;
     while (--i > -1) {
       if (this.hitTest(droppables[i], overlapThreshold)) {
         droppables[i].classList.add("red-border");
       } else {
         droppables[i].classList.remove("red-border");
       }
     }
   }
 }
});
```

You could also use hitTest() logic to detect if a mouseover happens, or any other kind of target.

We can write code like this from scratch with native methods, and use things like getBBox() or getBoundingClientRect() to calculate coordinate values. In fact, I'll show you how to work with some of these things for cool effects in Chapter 15. But if you're already loading and working with the Draggable plug-in for drag events, it makes sense to make use of the awesome utilities available to you.

Using Draggable to Control a Timeline

One of my favorite ways to work with Draggable is to pair it with other effects. Plotting a timeline with Draggable can create some beautiful scenes and give the user the power to control the progress. See Figure 12-2 and its corresponding example (*http://codepen.io/sdras/full/NqYGZv/*).

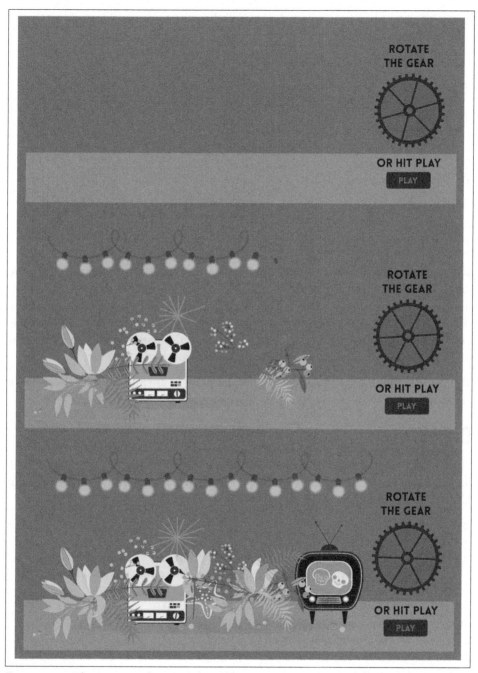

Figure 12-2. The user can choose to drag the scene in progressively by dragging the gear in rotation or by hitting play

In the interest of brevity, I'm not showing all the code to animate everything on the page here, but rather only focusing on how we're creating the interaction:

```
var master = new TimelineMax({paused:true});
master.add(sceneOne(), "scene1");

// master.seek("scene1");

Draggable.create(gear, {
  type: "rotation",
  bounds: {
    minRotation: 0,
    maxRotation: 360
  },
  onDrag: function() {
    master.progress((this.rotation)/360 );
  }
});
```

We pause the timeline initially, and then create a draggable instance of the gear. We define the bounds using `minRotation` and `maxRotation` so that the user can't keep dragging the gear forever. We also specify that the timeline will be plotted along the 360 degrees of the rotation using `progress()`. `progress()` is incredibly useful for this kind of timeline manipulation, because it allows you to create a range for the timeline's progress or manipulate events along certain points of the timeline.

You can also plot the interaction along straight lines, or anything else you like—there are so many possibilities!

DrawSVG

How would we make an SVG that looks like it's drawing itself on the page? Well, actually, we already learned this in Chapter 6 when we went over the Chartist with CSS animation example.

Loading Plug-ins

DrawSVG is a paid-for plug-in, but chances are you'll want to play with it before you spend money. GreenSock makes this possible by providing CodePen-safe versions of its plug-ins (*http://bit.ly/ 2lv1xhg*), which you can use in pens as you like.

Don't forget to load the plug-in resources and *TweenMax.min.js* into your pen before you get started.

Let's review this technique.

The first thing we need is an SVG element. This element has a stroke, and that stroke is dashed (see Figure 12-3).

Figure 12-3. Star shape with a dashed stroke

We can use a native method in JavaScript called .getTotalLength() to get the length of the shape:

```
var starID = document.getElementById('star');
console.log( starID.getTotalLength() );
```

We'll then set one of the dashes along the path, the stroke-dasharray, to the whole length of the shape (the integer we got from the console output). The *offset*, or stroke-dashoffset, is the distance into the pattern at which the start of the path is positioned. Since we're only setting one value for the array, it should be automatically duplicated so that gaps and dashes are equal in length. This is animatable, either with CSS without a framework or with JavaScript:

```
.path {
  stroke-dasharray: 1000;
  stroke-dashoffset: 1000;
  animation: dash 5s linear forwards;
}

@keyframes dash {
  to {
    stroke-dashoffset: 0;
  }
}
```

So, why would we use GreenSock to animate something that is easily animatable in CSS without a framework? Here are a few reasons:

- You're already loading GreenSock, and the plug-in allows you to animate these properties easily without calculating lengths.
- It'll work with regular rect, circle, ellipse, polyline, and polygon shapes, which don't have a .getTotalLength() method.
- The .getTotalLength() method is static and won't work on scaling SVGs that are adjusting responsively, whereas DrawSVG will.
- .getTotalLength() has some nasty bugs in IE and Firefox. If you just use it to console.log the value and then delete it, you can work around this problem, but not if you'd like to use this method to update dynamically.
- With GreenSock, you are not only able to animate from a beginning to an ending integer; you can use Booleans (true means fully drawn, false means not drawn at all) or percentages (my favorite!), or you can even have it animate in and collapse, with values like "50% 50%" (as both points start at 50%, they will not appear at all).

DrawSVG makes it easy to do very complex and stable animations, and when it's paired with other features like staggering, timelines, and relative HSL tweening (covered in the previous chapters), you can create beautiful effects easily, with only a single line of code:

```
TweenMax.staggerFromTo($draw, 4,{ drawSVG:'0' }, { drawSVG: true }, 0.1);
```

Figure 12-4 shows a more complex example (*http://bit.ly/2n7sUSP*), hinting at the possibilities.

EVERYTHING ON IT

Poem and Drawing by Shel Silverstein

I asked for a hot dog
With everything on it,
And that was my big mistake,
'Cause it came with a parrot,
A bee in a bonnet,
A wristwatch, a wrench, and a rake.
It came with a goldfish,
A flag, and a fiddle,
A frog, and a front porch swing,
And a mouse in a mask —
That's the last time I ask
For a hot dog with everything.

Figure 12-4. A demo showing a Shel Silverstein drawing being drawn onto the page while text is animated onto the page

Animate the Stroke!

With either CSS or DrawSVG, make sure the element has a stroke to begin with. I've seen students get stumped for a while because they didn't create a stroke initially—there was nothing to animate, so nothing happened, but nothing "failed" either.

This applies to groups too. If you target a group, make sure to get the elements *inside* the group, not just the group itself. Even if the stroke is applied to the group and then cascades to the other paths/shapes, the group *itself* doesn't have a stroke; only the elements do.

Working with DrawSVG is simple, and the multitude of ways to work with it make it really flexible and useful in a broad range of contexts.

CHAPTER 13

Mo.js

mo.js (*http://mojs.io/*) is a JavaScript library devoted to motion for the web. It offers a declarative syntax for motion and the creation of elements for animation. Even though mo.js is still in beta, there are already a host of amazing features to play with. Its author, Oleg Solomka (otherwise known as LegoMushroom), creates incredibly impressive demos and tutorials for the library's offerings that you should check out, but in this article we'll run through a really quick overview of features and tutorials to get you started.

Base Premises

mo.js basically offers two ways to make something that moves. You can do what other libraries do and reach inside the DOM or SVG DOM and move it, or you can create a special mo.js object, which has some unique offerings. There are fundamental things available to both ways of working, such as custom path easing and timelines. The path easing and timelines also have pretty impressive working tools to make them easier to adjust while you're working.

Shapes

Depending on what you're animating, the shapes and other objects that mo.js allows you to make might simplify your workflow. mo.js offers a declarative syntax that makes it very easy to create something on the fly.

Figure 13-1 and its corresponding example (*http://bit.ly/2hiKsG4*) are basic demos of the syntax.

Figure 13-1. A simple shape with a lot of nice details, including absolute centering

The code for this example is as follows:

```
var shape = new mojs.Shape({
    shape:       'circle', // shape "circle" is default
    radius:      50,
    fill:        '#A8CABA', // default is pink
    stroke:      '#5D4157',
    strokeWidth: 3,
    isShowStart: true,      // show before any animation starts
});
```

Here are some of the base things you need to know:

- The shapes that are available to you include circle, rect, cross, equal, zigzag, and polygon. (Default is circle).
- You define a fill, a stroke, and a strokeWidth. (Default is fill with no stroke or strokeWidth. equal and cross don't have space to fill, so they will not appear unless a stroke is specified.)
- You define a radius for the shape, and adjust it on an axis with an additional radiusX or radiusY. (Default is 50.)
- You let it know if you want to show the shape with isShowStart. This is a Boolean—true or false. true allows you to see it even if you're not going to animate the shape. (Default is false.)

- `polygon`, `zigzag.`, and `equal` allow you to pick a number of points so that you can create different types of shapes. (Default is 3.)
- All shapes will be placed relative to the middle of the screen using absolute positioning, unless you specify `top`, `left`, etc.

Figure 13-2 and its corresponding example (*http://bit.ly/2hfqThp*) demonstrate some of the shapes you can create.

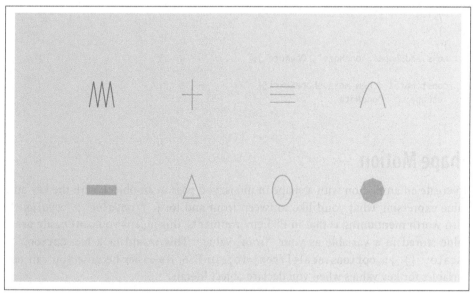

Figure 13-2. Some of the shapes that are available to you out of the box in mo.js

The code that creates the first shape (top left) is as follows:

```
const zigzag = new mojs.Shape({
    shape:       'zigzag',
    points:      7,
    radius:      25,
    radiusY:     50,
    top:         pos.row1,
    left:        pos.col1,
    fill:        'none',
    stroke:      color1,
    isShowStart: true,
});
```

You might notice if you look into the DOM that these are SVG shapes placed inside of a div for positioning. You can also pass a parent, like `parent: '#id-to-be-placed-under'`, if you'd like to put the shape somewhere within the DOM. You can pass any DOM node as a parent, so `parent: someEl` would work as well. At some point, you'll also be able to choose between using a div or SVG, which will be awesome, because it makes it much easier to create a scaling animation for mobile if you can place it with an SVG viewBox.

You can create custom shapes to animate as well, and add them in as the shape object:

```
// custom shape
class OneNote extends mojs.CustomShape {
  getShape () { return '<path d="M18.709
        ...
"/>';
  }
}
mojs.addShape( 'oneNote', OneNote );

const note1 = new mojs.ShapeSwirl({
  shape:     'oneNote',
  ...
});
```

Shape Motion

To create an animation with a shape in mo.js, you pass in an object, with the key and value expressing what you'd like to tween from and to: { *fromvalue* : *tovalue* }. Also worth mentioning is that in ES5 environments, this means you can't easily use a value stored in a variable as your "from" value. This would look like options = {scale: {} }; options.scale[from]=to;. In ES6, it's easier because you can use variables for key values when you declare object literals.

We can use transform properties like scale, angle (known in CSS as rotate), and opacity, and we can interpolate colors as well, as shown here with fill and in Figure 13-3:

```
scale:      { 0 : 1.5 },
angle:      { 0 : 180 },
fill:       { '#721e5f' : '#a5efce' },
```

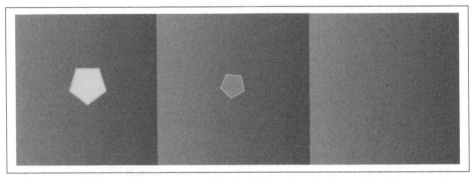

Figure 13-3. Shape tweens pass in an object to interpolate between two states

We can also specify a few other parameters:

- `duration`
- `delay`
- `repeat`
- `speed`—1 is the default speed, so `0.5` would be half speed and `1.5` would be 1.5× faster
- `isYoyo`—whether or not it tweens back and forth
- `easing`—written as an object, like `ease.in`, `ease.out`, or `ease.inout`
- `backwardEasing`—when using `isYoyo: true`, if you want the way that it eases back (on the backswing of the yoyo) to be different from the way that it eases forward, you would specify that with this method (defaults to `easing` if not specified)
- `isSoftHide`—whether it hides the shape with transforms rather than `display` (Boolean, defaults to `true`)

Easy Random Generation

In other JavaScript libraries, we'd either write a helper function to use random values, or use a bit of code that allows us to pick the ceiling and floor values to choose between. (See the note in the opening section of Chapter 11 for more details on `Math.random()`.)

In mo.js, we can abstract this away very nicely. We can pass in *random values* by writing the string *property* : `'rand(min, max)'`; for instance, `angle: 'rand(0, 360)'`.

Chaining

If we'd like to chain two animations on a `Shape`, we can call `.then()` on the initial tween, like so (*http://bit.ly/2gwtmpo*):

```
const polygon = new mojs.Shape({
    shape:      'polygon',
    points:     5,
    stroke:     '#A8CABA',
    scale:      { 0 : 1.5 },
    angle:      { 0 : 180 },
    fill:       { '#721e5f' : '#a5efce' },
    radius:     25,
    duration:   1200,
    easing:     'sin.out'
}).then ({
    stroke:     '#000',
    angle:      [-360],
    scale:      0,
```

```
    easing:        'sin.in'
  });
```

Swirls

Features like ShapeSwirl and Burst are interesting parts of mo.js; they're pretty beautiful out of the box. A ShapeSwirl is similar to a regular Shape object, but the movement is pretty much how it sounds—the shape swirls around. You have a few parameters to work with for a swirl, and they are all based on the sine that the swirl works with:

- swirlSize—the amount it swirls horizontally (the deviation or amplitude of the sine)
- swirlFrequency—the frequency of the sine
- pathScale—the scale (length) of the sine
- degreeShift—the angle of the sine, used if you'd like to make it move toward a different direction on a 360 degree plane (especially useful for using ShapeSwirl with a Burst)
- direction—the direction of the sine, either -1 or 1 (good for setting something in the other direction if you want it to look a little random)
- isSwirl—whether the shape should follow a sinusoidal path (Boolean—true or false)

These can be a little confusing to read and grok, so I've made a demo (*http://codepen.io/sdras/full/mrZWqg/*) so you can play with the values to understand them a little better. Figure 13-4 is a screenshot of the demo.

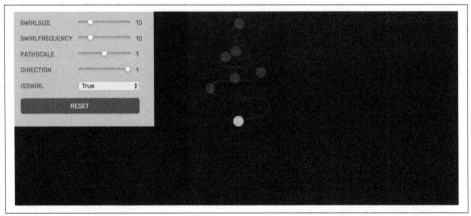

Figure 13-4. Playing with the controls in this demo shows how all of the built-in options for a mo.js ShapeSwirl work

Also, you can set up a few base configurations—like a custom shape, or an object, with some configuration—to reuse for different ShapeSwirls (or any other shape) with an ES6 spread operator like this (*http://codepen.io/sdras/pen/OReWOw*) (Figure 13-5). This is really nice if you have a few similar objects:

```
const note_opts_two = {
    shape:      'twoNote',
    scale:      { 5 : 20 },
    y:          { 20: -10 },
    duration: 3000,
    easing: 'sin.out'
};

const note1 = new mojs.ShapeSwirl({
    ...note_opts_two,
    fill:      { 'cyan' : color2 },
    swirlSize:        15,
    swirlFrequency: 20
}).then({
    opacity:  0,
    duration: 200,
    easing: 'sin.in'
});
```

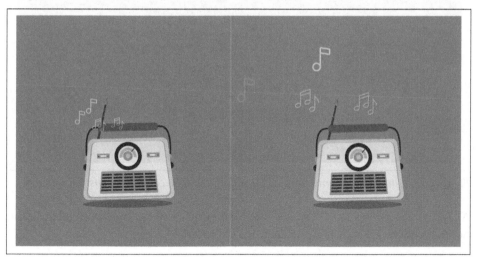

Figure 13-5. This demo shows ShapeSwirl used for the motion of the notes

Burst

A Burst is also really quite lovely out of the box. If you use the default configuration, you would say this:

```
const burst = new mojs.Burst().play();
```

To configure a `Burst`, you have a few options (*http://codepen.io/sdras/pen/kkqNYK*), as shown in Figure 13-6:

- `count`—the number of children in the `Burst` (default is 5)
- `degree`—the number of degrees around the center that the children come from
- `radius`—the radius that the children spread out to (`radiusX` and `radiusY` apply here as well)
- `isSoftHide`—whether it hides the children with transforms rather than `display` (Boolean, defaults to `true`); this applies to *all* shapes, but I bring it up again because it's particularly useful for a `Burst` with several children

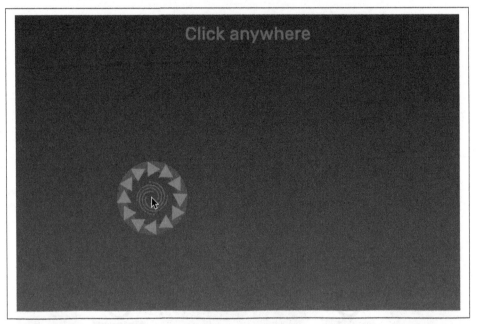

Figure 13-6. You can customize quite a lot in a Burst: size, color, even custom shapes

All of the same rules for `Shape` also apply to `Burst`, and we can apply them to the nodes themselves as a separate object using `children`, like this:

```
const burst = new mojs.Burst({
  radius: { 0: 100 },
  count: 12,
  children: {
    shape: 'polygon',
    ...
  }
});
```

Timeline

In a `Timeline`, you can either `.add` a bunch of objects or tweens that you have previously declared as a variable, or you can `.append` them, and have them fall in order:

```
const timeline = new mojs.Timeline({
  .add( tween )
  .append( tween )
});
```

`.add`: allows you to add any objects or shapes to the timeline. They'll all fire at once, but you can still use delays or staggering to adjust their timing. `.append`: adds objects, but staggers them in the order they are added.

There are a few things you can do in a `Timeline` that are worth noting. You can add `repeat`, `delay`, and `speed`, just like to the objects themselves, as object parameters, like this:

```
new mojs.Timeline({
  repeat: 3,
  isYoyo: true
});
```

You can also nest a `Timeline` inside another `Timeline`; you can even nest them infinitely:

```
const subTimeline = new mojs.Timeline();

const master = new mojs.Timeline()
.add( subTimeline );
```

Tween

With all of these constructors, we haven't really spoken too much about tweening (animating) what already exists. All of the same parameters for shape motion (`duration`, `repeat`, `easing`, etc.) are also available for `Tween`s. To use a `Tween`, we update styles or attributes (whatever we're trying to change) along a path. Here's a simple example:

```
var thingtoselect = document.querySelector('#thingtoselect');
new mojs.Tween({
  duration:    2000,
  onUpdate: function (progress) {
    square.style.transform = 'translateY(' + 200*progress + 'px)';
  }
}).play();
```

I used this kind of tween to create the effect on the far left side of the example (*http://codepen.io/sdras/pen/JRQXGz*) in Figure 13-7, of the little zigzags drawing themselves on repeatedly using the SVG line drawing trick (*http://bit.ly/2l8ns1m*) with stroke-dashoffset. I'm also using the path easing available in mo.js, which is discussed in the next section. I made the water in the tanks appear to move by updating SVG path attributes as well.

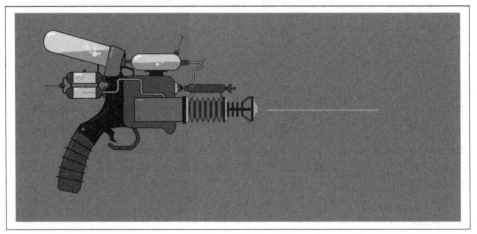

Figure 13-7. Raygun with mo.js swirls and path easing

Here's the code for the laser beam:

```
new mojs.Tween({
  repeat:   999,
  duration: 2000,
  isYoyo: true,
  isShowEnd: false,
  onUpdate: function (progress) {
    var laser1EProgress = laser1E(progress);
    for (var i = 0; i < allSideL.length; i++) {
      allSideL[i].style.strokeDashoffset = 20*laser1EProgress + '%';
      allSideL[i].style.opacity = Math.abs(0.8*laser1EProgress);
    }
  }
}).play();
```

Tweens have rich callbacks available that take into account fine-tuning that can sometimes make all the difference. Some examples of this are `onStart` versus `onRepeat Start`, `onComplete` versus `onRepeatComplete`, and `onPlaybackStart` versus `onPlaybackPause`. A full list is available in the docs (*http://bit.ly/2lKXq1z*).

Path Easing

A very cool feature of mo.js is that aside from the other built-in easing values (*http:// bit.ly/2mkI5aR*), you can also pass in an SVG path as an easing value. I use this feature in several demos in this chapter, but to be honest, I could never do path easing justice like the gorgeous tutorial LegoMushroom has prepared (*http://mojs.io/tutorials/*

easing/path-easing/). I'll simply explain the base premises to get you started and show you how it works, but I highly recommend going through his post.

Before we go through all of path easing, it's important to establish that if you'd like to work with something out of the box, the base functions will get you very far. The syntax for built-in easing is written like so:

```
easing: 'cubic.in'
```

Mastering easing can be the key ingredient to bringing your animations to life, so being able to fine-tune your motion with custom paths is helpful. If you're comfortable animating in CSS, you might like the mo.js `bezier` easing, which accepts the same curve values (without some of the same restrictions), as CSS's `cubic-bezier` (*http://cubic-bezier.com/*). Here's an example of this kind of easing:

```
easing: 'bezier( 0.910, 0.000, 0.110, 1.005 )'
```

If you'd like more refined control than what `bezier` easing allows, path easing is really nice. You pass in an SVG path, and your shape is updated to work with it. Let's look back again at the example I pulled out earlier from the raygun. I used path easing to interpolate the values as it updated:

```
const laser1E = mojs.easing.path('M0,400S58,111.1,80.5,175.1s43,286.4,
              63,110.4,46.3-214.8,70.8-71.8S264.5,369,285,225.5s16.6-209.7,
              35.1-118.2S349.5,258.5,357,210,400,0,400,0');

new mojs.Tween({
  repeat:   999,
  duration: 2000,
  isYoyo: true,
  isShowEnd: false,
  onUpdate: function (progress) {
    var laser1EProgress = laser1E(progress);
    for (var i = 0; i < allSideL.length; i++) {
      allSideL[i].style.strokeDashoffset = 20*laser1EProgress + '%';
      allSideL[i].style.opacity = Math.abs(0.8*laser1EProgress);
    }
  }
}).play();
```

To really get a sense of how a path ease can affect the movement and behavior of an animation, check out the CodePen demo in the next section. The curve editor tool that mo.js offers will help you to visualize and immediately get a sense of how an ease can refine what you create.

Mo.js Tools

One of the most impressive things about mo.js is the tooling. To whet your palate, there is a demonstration on Vimeo (*https://vimeo.com/185587462*); see Figure 13-8.

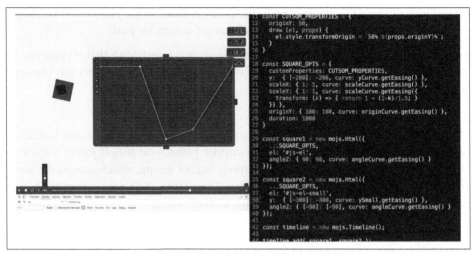

```
11  const CUTSOM_PROPERTIES = {
12    originY: 50,
13    draw (el, props) {
14      el.style.transformOrigin = `50% ${props.originY}%`;
15    }
16  }
17
18  const SQUARE_OPTS = {
19    customProperties: CUTSOM_PROPERTIES,
20    y: { [-200]: -200, curve: yCurve.getEasing() },
21    scaleX: { 1: 1, curve: scaleCurve.getEasing() },
22    scaleY: { 1: 1, curve: scaleCurve.getEasing({
23      transform: (k) => { return 1 + (1-k)/1.5; }
24    }) },
25    originY: { 100: 100, curve: originCurve.getEasing() },
26    duration: 1000
27  }
28
29  const square1 = new mojs.Html({
30    ...SQUARE_OPTS,
31    el: '#js-el',
32    angleZ: { 90: 90, curve: angleCurve.getEasing() }
33  });
34
35  const square2 = new mojs.Html({
36    ...SQUARE_OPTS,
37    el: '#js-el-small',
38    y: { [-300]: -300, curve: ySmall.getEasing() },
39    angleZ: { [-90]: [-90], curve: angleCurve.getEasing() }
40  });
41
42  const timeline = new mojs.Timeline();
43
44  timeline.add( square1, square2 );
```

Figure 13-8. Mo.js workflow demo on Vimeo

I made a quick pen to showcase both the player tool and the curve editor so that you can play around with them (Figure 13-9). Feel free to either fork it or just adjust it live in CodePen (*http://bit.ly/2gqz2mo*); it's fun to try out. The curve tool is on the left side and the timeline is tucked at the bottom with a little arrow.

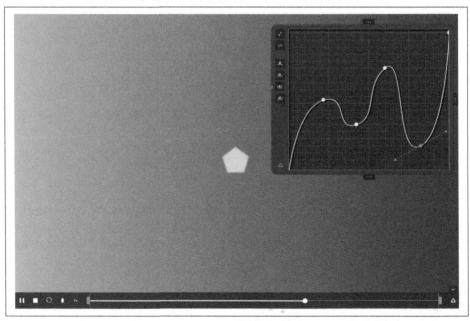

Figure 13-9. This is a starter pen you can easily fork to play around with mo.js tooling

Here's the coolest part: LegoMushroom isn't done. He's working on new tooling for the timeline now. Check out the awesome design for this tool on GitHub (*http://bit.ly/2mtJuZN*). If you're interested in contributing to open source, here's an opportunity to dig in and help make a really useful tool—click on the "help wanted" label on the right!

The other finished tools are available in their own repos:

- Player: *http://bit.ly/2lv7wT9*
- Curve editor: *http://bit.ly/2mHhW2f*

There is also a Slack channel (*https://hamsterpad.com/chat/mojs*) you can join if you're interested in contributing or learning.

If you're the kind of person who likes playing with things more than reading, all of the CodePen demos from this chapter are available in a collection (*http://codepen.io/collection/XOEKow/*).

There are, of course, things in the library that I didn't cover in this chapter. I went over some of the most useful features of mo.js in my opinion, but there are more things to discover. Check out the docs (*http://bit.ly/2lkK6ie*) for more information.

CHAPTER 14

React-Motion

There are many ways to animate an SVG in React, and any one of the techniques we've covered can be altered and used in a React context. But React-Motion (*http://bit.ly/2lSUy2l*) has some beautiful offerings that make it stand out, making it worthwhile to spend a chapter focusing on the features.

As mentioned in Chapter 7, React-Motion is very different from sequentially based sequencing techniques such as CSS or the GreenSock timeline, in that we aren't actually using time to control our interpolation at all.

Like with game-based physics, with React-Motion we give our elements mass and spring parameters, and send them on their way. For this reason, we can get very lifelike motion that is *interruptible* (I'll explain what I mean by this in a moment), and can create incredibly beautiful motion in a UI.

React-Motion exports three main components: `<Motion/>`, `<StaggeredMotion/>`, and `<TransitionMotion/>`.

But the full list of exports includes the following:

- `spring`
- `Motion`
- `StaggeredMotion`
- `TransitionMotion`
- `presets`

We're mainly going to focus on the `<Motion />` and `<StaggeredMotion />` components in this chapter, but there is more information available in the README of the project (*https://github.com/chenglou/react-motion*).

Getting up to Speed

If you aren't accustomed to React or ES6, this chapter might be confusing for you. My suggestion is to get to grips with the working principles each of these first (which is out of the scope of this book), and then return here to learn more about React-Motion as an animation library. You can't use React-Motion without React, so understanding the base premises are important before continuing.

<Motion />

We'll start with the <Motion /> component that React-Motion makes available to you.

In these examples, we'll be using integers passed through styles to change the appearance of something over time. Truly, you can animate any two values, be it a number in a path or a color value; it's just most common to use the style pattern. Also, browsers are pretty good at changing some style properties without incurring many layout triggers (namely transforms and opacity), as we covered in Chapter 2, so we'll take advantage of that.

Let's break down how we implement this step by step before going over some demo code. In this example (*http://bit.ly/2iFJCG7*), we'll just update some integers so you can see what's happening (Figure 14-1).

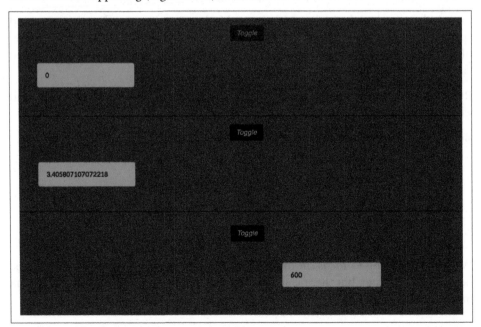

Figure 14-1. Interpolating a number as well as a transform

First, our initial state will be a simple Boolean:

```
getInitialState() {
  return {open: false};
},
```

Then we'll change the state based on a mouse click or touch of a button:

```
handleMouseDown() {
    this.setState({open: !this.state.open});
},

handleTouchStart(e) {
    e.preventDefault();
    this.handleMouseDown();
},
```

In our render method, we'll have a button that calls the methods we just defined to update the state:

```
<button
  onMouseDown={this.handleMouseDown}
  onTouchStart={this.handleTouchStart}>
  Toggle
</button>
```

Then we'll use the `<Motion />` component made available to us through React-Motion to both update the integer and update the transform style directly on the div that contains it. Consider the fact that any time you use a library like GSAP, you're setting inline styles with JavaScript under the hood. This isn't that much different, even if they are written in a different way:

```
<Motion style={{x: spring(this.state.open ? 600 : 0)}}>
  {
    ({x}) =>
      <div className="simple-demo" style={{
        WebkitTransform: `translate3d(${x}px, 0, 0)`,
        transform: `translate3d(${x}px, 0, 0)`,
      }}>{x}</div>
  }
</Motion>
```

I've split apart some of the syntax onto separate lines just so you can see it a little more clearly. We start by creating a `style` object that takes x as a key (you can use anything you wish here) and sets the value to a ternary operator set by whether the state of open is `true` or `false`.

We then pass that x value down, and are able to use it as a variable for whatever interpolation we wish. Here we have the style, created with ES6 template literals for legibility. Take care here, as unlike with GreenSock, where the prefixes are handled for us, you have to write out the prefixes you need—in this case, one for WebKit for the `transform` property.

I've also placed just the x variable inside the div {x} so that you can see the numbers update along with the style moving it across.

Color and React-Motion Interpolation

Unlike styles like position properties, SVG path units, or opacity, some properties do not accept values that aren't full numbers. Color is one such example, when you write it as a hexadecimal or RGBA value. (For example, there is no color for `rbga(33.2428797, 47, 52, 1)`.) There are some workarounds here, though. You can either concatenate a `%` at the end of these numbers, or you can use a `Math.floor()`/`Math.round()` to get around this. You can also use `hsla()`, which is interpreting a full hue (h) rotation—quite lovely because it never fails, even when going above 360—or a percentage for s and l values.

Decimal points for color components *will* be supported in the future, as the color space for web pages expands beyond sRGB to DCI-P3 and other wider gamuts.

Now that we have the basics down, lets animate an SVG!

Take a look at Figure 14-2 and its corresponding example (*http://codepen.io/sdras/pen/ZWeJem*).

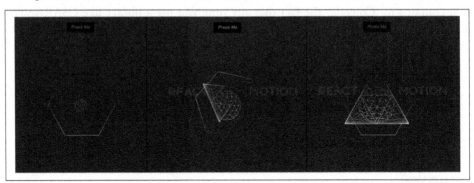

Figure 14-2. The SVG rotates in and the text draws on when you toggle

Here's a pared-down version of the code it takes to run the demo, so that you can see what's going on a little more easily:

```
<Motion style={{
    // designate all of the differences in interpolated values in these
    // ternary operators
    ...
    dash: spring(this.state.compact ? 0 : 200),
    rotate: spring(this.state.compact ? 0 : 180),
```

```
    ...
  }}>
  {/* make sure the values are passed below */} {({dash, rotate, ...}) =>
    <svg viewBox="0 0 803.9 738.1" aria-labelledby="title">
      <title>React-Motion</title>
      <g>
        <path
          style={{
          WebkitTransform: `scale(${scale}) rotate(${rotate}deg)`,
          transform: `scale(${scale}) rotate(${rotate}deg)` }}
          className="polygon cls-2"
          d="M529.8,359.7l-25.1-43.5-25.4-43.9-25.7-44.4L428,183.3..." />
      </g>
      ...
      <g style={{ strokeDashoffset: `${dash}` }}
        className="react-letters"
        data-name="react motion letters">
          <path className="cls-5" d="M178.4,247a2.2,2.2,0,0,1,1-3.5,
          2.6l-6.5-8.7h-8.6v7.4a2.2,2.2,0,0,1-4.4,0V220.1a2.2,2.2,
          0,0,1,2.2-2.2h10.8a11.5,11.5,0,0,1,4.8,22Zm-18.6-10.3h8.6a7.3,
          7.3,0,0,0,0-14.7h-8.6v14.7Z" transform="translate(3.1 1.5)" />
          ...
      </g>
    </svg>
  }
</Motion>
```

We're using pretty much the same logic here, with a toggle that will change the state (this time referenced by the key compact, or this.state.compact). You can see how we change the values for different style properties in the <Motion /> component— you can actually pass a variety of values. For instance, for the stroke-dashoffset, a technique we described in both Chapters 6 and 12, we'll need to change the value of the dashoffset to the length of the shape—in this case, 200:

```
dash: spring(this.state.compact ? 0 : 200)
```

rotate will alternate in 180-degree segments:

```
rotate: spring(this.state.compact ? 0 : 180)
```

Now we're able to plot the change in state of styles over the spring. We can apply it to any path, and even to groups, as shown in the preceding example. We've inlined the SVG here directly in the JSX. All SVG properties are supported as of v15—see the pull request from zpao (*https://github.com/facebook/react/pull/6243*) that I'm hugely grateful for. The only exception is that we have placed the gradient we will use repeatedly for the sections directly in the HTML, because it helps with *render speed and performance* (as we're not wrapping all of the individual tags under the hood with React.createElement()):

```
<svg width="0" height="0" xmlns="http://www.w3.org/2000/svg"
    xmlns:xlink="http://www.w3.org/1999/xlink" viewBox="0 0
                      803.9 738.1">
  <defs>
    <linearGradient id="linear-gradient" x1="399.74" y1="370.41"
      x2="399.74" y2="134.33" gradientUnits="userSpaceOnUse">
      <stop offset="0" stop-color="#fff"/>
      <stop offset="1"/>
    </linearGradient>
    <linearGradient id="linear-gradient-2" x1="406.42"
      y1="415.63" x2="406.42" y2="166.91" xlink:href="#linear-gradient"/>
  </defs>
</svg>
```

You'll also notice I've collapsed the height and width of the SVG containing the gradient—nothing should render to the DOM with a gradient, but some browsers will show a bit of space here, so we do this for some added insurance. I can then call the ID of #linear-gradient inside of SVG that's in JSX whenever I wish and it will be available to me.

A Note on Performance

Rendering an SVG with JavaScript is ever so slightly more costly. My rule of thumb is that if it's under a few KB, it's generally not that noticeable, but anything above that, and you should try to make an SVG sprite and reuse it in the JSX with <use>. The <use> tag comes with its own strange animation issues, so it's best to avoid this for anything but icons or images that won't move. Inlining just the SVG that needs to move around with state changes is my personal recommendation, but I'm happy to hear others as well. Whatever you try, be sure to test, both with the JS timeline in dev tools and also visually, with real users.

Interruptible Motion

One thing to note in the demo is that you can reverse it midstream: it is interruptible. If you recall, with some of the other technologies that we covered that are sequentially based, what you're working with is *time*. React-Motion never mentions time at all.

> Animation APIs parameterized by eg duration and curve are fundamentally opposed to continuous, fluid interactivity.
>
> —Andy Matuschak (*http://bit.ly/2lQv5Jf*)

The mechanics of this library, and the game-based physics mentioned earlier, give us the ability to interrupt it. In a simple toggle, that might not seem like much to write home about. But what if you're working with a menu that opens and closes? If the user decides to close it while it's opening and has to wait for it to finish, then give it a tap again, this will feel like an error. It's subtle, but noticeable.

Does this mean that interruptible motion is superior? In one way, yes; in other ways, no. Both sequentially timed and interruptible motion have their place.

In some of the other demos we've explored (for example, the SplitText demo (*http:// codepen.io/sdras/pen/RNWaMX*), "Turn it Around" from Chapter 11), or my pen (*http://codepen.io/sdras/pen/dPqRmP*) "When you're an introvert," this kind of fluidity wouldn't make any sense. Aside from the fact that you can't write a loop in React-Motion without writing an infinite loop (please don't do that, unless you work on a site that harms children or puppies—then you should definitely do that), writing an animation that makes use of timing and sequence without tools that make the fine-tuning of sequence available to you would be silly. And not good silly, like whiskey poured on ice cream.

On the other hand, if you had a stream of chat heads you had to move around the screen and collapse in order to keep typing a message, that would be a *perfect* time to use React-Motion, or a library that shares these principles. Not only would it work *well*, it would work *beautifully*.

The `<StaggeredMotion />` component shows the benefits of this type of motion the best, so we'll dive into that next.

`<StaggeredMotion />`

When I covered staggers previously, the effect could be summarized as: "Here is a group of elements. I want to change them over a certain number of seconds, by updating a property *this* much. But I want them to each fire a little bit after one another." The `<StaggeredMotion />` component in React-Motion doesn't quite work the same way.

We've covered how we're not using time-based sequencing. So how would we fire things consecutively? Especially when the motion is interruptible? What happens is we send something on its way, and then update the next sibling's placement based on where the first one is headed. In essence, it gets the motion "for free."

This way, when you drag something around and update its placement, the elements don't just go with it; they scatter behind it in a really beautiful way. If you couple that with some of the spring parameter features (which we will), the effect can be quite lovely, as shown in Figure 14-3 and its corresponding example (*http://codepen.io/ sdras/pen/pyedJE*).

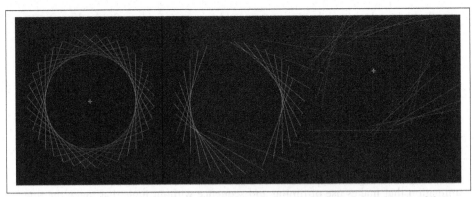

Figure 14-3. When you drag the staggered component around, you get a sense of the interruptible motion, and the difference in the way that it staggers

If you look at only one demo on the web from this book, this is the one you should check out, because it's really hard to describe the motion without seeing it. Let's break down the code.

In getInitialState(), we have an object that starts the circle off at 250 or the x coordinate (pageX) and 300 for the y. Part of the reason we do that is so that viewers can see the cascade when they first visit the page and the circle orientation isn't off to the top left of the page. We also set rotate to 0.

When the component mounts, we listen for both mouse and touch input (for desktop and mobile), calling different functions to set the state of the placement of the x and y to the center of that input:

```
getInitialState() {
  return {x: 250, y: 300, rotate:0};
},

componentDidMount() {
  window.addEventListener('mousemove', this.handleMouseMove);
  window.addEventListener('touchmove', this.handleTouchMove);
},

// we're setting the state to be equal to the position
handleMouseMove({pageX: x, pageY: y}) {
  this.setState({x, y});
},

handleTouchMove({touches}) {
  this.handleMouseMove(touches[0]);
},
```

In the next method, getStyles(), we set the styles from the previous style placement. Note that this doesn't occur within the render() method, and we have to pass in the original styles as a parameter.

We're also doing something we didn't do in the previous <Motion /> component (but could have if we wanted to): we're designating a stiffness and dampening. This will change the way that the spring physics of React-Motion behaves, and how siblings will inherit the motion in tandem:

```
getStyles(prevStyles) {
    // we're using the previous style to update the next one's placement
    const endValue = prevStyles.map((_, i) => {
      let stiff = 200, damp = 15;
      return i === 0
        ? this.state
        : {
            x: spring(prevStyles[i - 1].x, {stiffness: stiff, damping: damp}),
            y: spring(prevStyles[i - 1].y, {stiffness: stiff, damping: damp}),
            rotate: spring((i * 10), {stiffness: stiff, damping: damp})
          };
    });
    return endValue;
},
```

React-Motion has a nice demo page (*http://bit.ly/2hWextu*) where you can play around with all of these parameters.

Now, in the <StaggeredMotion /> component, we start initially with the default styles that we've pushed onto the array, which will update to styles and the state as soon as the component is mounted (which creates the initial cascade). After that, we divide the length of lines in half for the x and y values so that we can be sure that the touch or mouse input will be in the center of the ring. We also rotate the whole circle for effect, by the i*10 specified in the getStyles() method:

```
render() {
  let arr = [], amtHalf = 175;
  for (var i = 0; i < 50; i++) {
    arr.push({x: 0, y:0, rotate:0});
  }
  return (
    <div>
      <StaggeredMotion
        defaultStyles = {arr}
        styles={this.getStyles}>
        {lines =>
          <div className="demo">
            {lines.map(({x, y, rotate}, i) =>
              <div
                key={i}
                className={`playthings s${i}`}
```

```
            // we have to subtract half the amount of $amt in
            // the CSS panel so that the mouse stays in the
            // center of the object we're creating
            style={{
              WebkitTransform: `translate3d(${x - amtHalf}px,
                ${y - amtHalf}px, 0) rotate(${rotate}deg)`,
              transform: `translate3d(${x - amtHalf}px,
                ${y - amtHalf}px, 0) rotate(${rotate}deg)`
            }} />
          )}
        </div>
      }
    </StaggeredMotion>
  </div>
);
},
```

The result is a really fun and fluid interactive animation that can change direction on a user's whim.

CHAPTER 15

Animating the Unanimatable: Motion with Attributes and Bare-Metal Implementations

One of the great powers of working with JavaScript for animation over CSS is that we aren't limited by what CSS considers animatable. There are a lot of attributes that can create amazing effects when interpolated, and certainly several more where this hasn't even been attempted in any real way yet.

requestAnimationFrame()

Of course, you don't need a library at all to animate an SVG. One nice and perform- ant way of animating is to use `requestAnimationFrame()` (rAF for short). rAF can be used as a replacement for other native methods, like `setInterval()` (though this method has been improved by backporting features that rAF pioneered).

The way it works is you tell the browser a function that updates the animation prior to the next repaint. rAF calls do not create a nested call stack, which can be a perfor- mance problem. Instead, they add the callback to the queue managed by the browser, and only one instance of the function is ever running at a given time.

The magic of `requestAnimationFrame()` is that it will run at 60 frames per second when it can, but under the hood, it will actually figure out how fast to run based on your device: it will run faster on desktop and slower on mobile. It will also stop work- ing when running in a background tab, so battery life is preserved, and it doesn't use resources when it doesn't need them. This saves us work as developers—all of this used to have to be manually handled in `setInterval()`, as we'd have to declare time deltas for different browsers or inactive tabs.

Browser Support for rAF

You used to need to use browser prefixes and polyfills for `requestAnimationFrame()`, but luckily, support has climbed, and this is now only necessary if you need to support IE9 or older. Opera Mini does not support rAF at all, but it also doesn't run any JS client-side. It just builds your site on the proxy server from your initial JS and then sends that to the user. Just keep in mind that Opera Mini browsing is basically like seeing a screenshot/PDF of a web page.

The syntax for rAF looks like this:

```
function animateSVG() {
  // here is where your animation code would go
  requestAnimationFrame(animateSVG);
}
requestAnimationFrame(animateSVG);
```

You can also use rAF in an IIFE (immediately invoked function expression):

```
(function animate() {
  requestAnimationFrame(animate);
}());
```

Of course, you don't have to put all of the code for the animation inside the function —you can also call another function that invokes the animation updates. The callback here would usually be dependent on some sort of test to decide whether the animation is already "finished" (unless you want an infinite looping animation).

In the following demo (Figure 15-1), I created an object pool with SVG circles. If you'll recall, drawing SVG circles takes three attributes: r, for radius; cx, which plots the middle of the circle on the x-axis in the coordinate system; and cy, which plots the circle on the y-axis. In this demo (*http://bit.ly/2hL5UFs*), we'll update the placement of the circle with cx and cy values—two attributes that currently aren't animatable properties in CSS.

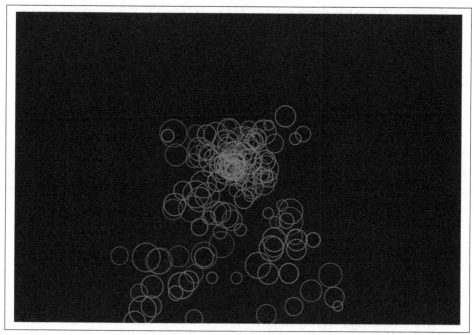

Figure 15-1. A particle fountain built with an object pool that updates SVG attributes with requestAnimationFrame()

In this example, we first declare our variables and then drum up the attributes. We set the width and height to the size of the page using .innerWidth and .innerHeight (which get the page's height and width) and use these values to create our viewBox. We also define some gravity, friction, and an empty object to use later on:

```
var svg = document.createElementNS("http://www.w3.org/2000/svg", "svg"),
    svgNS = svg.namespaceURI,
    vbx = document.createElementNS(svgNS, "viewBox"),
    width = window.innerWidth,
    height = window.innerHeight,
    gravity = 0.00009,
    friction = 0.000001,
    lots = [],
    prevTime;

document.body.appendChild(svg);
document.body.style.background = '#222';
svg.setAttribute("viewBox", "0 0 " + width + " " + height);
svg.setAttribute("width", width);
svg.setAttribute("height", height);
```

Correct Namespacing

Because SVG is written in a different namespace, creating elements has a slight gotcha. You must use `document.createElementNS()`, using the SVG namespace URL, which you can always access from the `.namespaceURI` property of any existing SVG element. I usually create a variable for this, shown in the preceding code as `svgNS = svg.namespaceURI`, in order to cache it and quickly reuse it.

We can now create the bubble with an object constructor function that defines the initial state of an object created with `new Bubble()`. This takes two arguments: the two things about the bubble that we want to randomize, `opacity` and `radius`. We also append it to the SVG in the middle of the `viewBox`:

```
function Bubble(opacity, radius) {
    this.init(width/2, height/2, 0, 0);
    this.opacity = opacity;
    this.radius = radius;
    var circ = document.createElementNS(svgNS, "circle");
    svg.appendChild(circ);
    circ.setAttribute("r", this.radius);
    circ.setAttribute("fill", "none");
    circ.setAttribute("stroke-width", "1px");
    this.circ = circ;
}
```

We can then create an object prototype that defines two shared methods for all `Bubble` objects—the `init()` method that is used to set an initial position and velocity, and the `update()` method that updates the placement of the bubble based on acceleration, friction (which slows the velocity), and gravity (all formulas learned from physics texts and modified, written out in comments here):

```
Bubble.prototype = {
    init: function (x, y, vx, vy) {
        this.x = x;
        this.y = y;
        this.vx = vx;
        this.vy = vy;
    },
    update: function (dt) {
        // friction opposes the direction of velocity
        var acceleration = -Math.sign(this.vx) * friction;
        // distance = velocity * time + 0.5 * acceleration * (time ^ 2)
        this.x += this.vx * dt + 0.5 * acceleration * (dt ^ 2);
        this.y += this.vy * dt + 0.5 * gravity * (dt ^ 2);
        // velocity = velocity + acceleration * time
        this.vy += gravity * dt;
        this.vx += acceleration * dt;
        this.circ.setAttribute("cx", this.x);
        this.circ.setAttribute("cy", this.y);
```

```
      this.circ.setAttribute("stroke", "rgba(1,146,190," + this.opacity + ")");
    }
  };
```

We are calling `init()` twice for each bubble. Once, the constructor creates them centered and still, and then a separate method call randomizes the speed. We can initiate the `Bubbles` with some parameters for the opacity and radius, and also push them onto the array we created earlier (I called it `lots` because sometimes it's hard to name things—you can yell at me on Twitter about it if you like, but full disclosure: I'll probably send you a GIF of a cat frowning in response):

```
for (var i = 0; i < 150; i++) {
  setTimeout(function () {
    var single = new Bubble(0.5+Math.random()*0.5, 5 + Math.random()*10);
    initBubble(single);
    lots.push(single);
  }, i*18);
}

...

function initBubble(single) {
  single.init(width/2, height/2, -0.05 + Math.random()*0.1, -0.1 + Math.random()
  *0.1);
}
```

We then use `requestAnimationFrame()` to cycle through the `lots` of `Bubbles` array and activate it, redrawing all of the positions using the `update()` method we defined in the `Bubble` object prototype. We've made some small adjustments here, because if the height of the page is really small we can allow the circles to fall all the way down before updating them, but otherwise we should update more often:

```
(function animate(currentTime) {
  var dt;
  requestAnimationFrame(animate);
  if (!prevTime) {
    // only save previous time
    prevTime = currentTime;
    return;
  } else {
    // calculate the time difference between frames;
    // if it's more than 25 ms, assume it's because the tab
    // wasn't active, and just use 25 ms
    dt = Math.min(currentTime - prevTime, 25);
    prevTime = currentTime;
  }
  for (var i = 0; i < lots.length; i++) {
    lots[i].update(dt);

    // if the height is small, just let it start over when it gets to the bottom;
    // otherwise, at 85% (so that there aren't big gaps)
```

```
      if (height < 500) {
        if (lots[i].y > height) {
          initBubble(lots[i]);
        }
      } else {
        if (lots[i].y > height*0.85) {
          initBubble(lots[i]);
        }
      }
    }
  }());
```

With `requestAnimationFrame()` we have a lot of flexibility in how we can build our animations without adding any additional resources. We can also animate properties that aren't in the spec. Indeed, most JavaScript animation libraries use rAF under the hood, so if you want to get close to understanding animations without abstraction, building some with rAF is a good way to go.

Keep in mind that the abstractions that some libraries offer are useful for keeping your code DRY, legible, and clean, so in production environments, it might make more sense to use a library, but every site is different and has different requirements.

GreenSock's AttrPlugin

GreenSock's AttrPlugin comes baked into TweenMax (see Chapter 8), so you don't need to add in any additional resources beyond *TweenMax.min.js*. The syntax for `attr` is slightly different than for the animatable properties:

```
TweenMax.to(".trial", 3, {
  attr: {
    d: "M 100 300 C 125 200 175 200 200 100 Q 250 550 300 300
    Q 350 50 400 450 C 450 550 450 50 500 300
    C 550 50 550 550 600 200 A 50 50 0 1 1 700 300"
  },
  ease: Expo.easeOut
});
```

You can see how we nest the properties to be animated inside `attr`, unlike with other properties. For the other animatable properties that follow, we use them outside the `attr` object:

```
TweenMax.to(".trial", 3, {
  attr: {
    d: "M 100 300 C 125 200 175 200 200 100 Q 250 550 300 300 Q 350 50 400 450 C
    450 550 450 50 500 300 C 550 50 550 550 600 200 A 50 50 0 1 1 700 300"
  },
  x: 300,
  ease: Expo.easeOut
});
```

You can see that I used this to tween a path value here. It's easy enough to do if you have the same amount of path points; you don't necessarily need MorphSVG (Chapter 10). In fact, you can create some fairly sophisticated path effects by tweening path values if you take the time to understand them.

There are other things we can now tween as well. For example, we can create an animated gradient mask (*http://bit.ly/2h77stW*) with this JavaScript:

```
TweenMax.fromTo("#stop1", 1.5, {
  attr:{offset:-1}
}, {
  attr:{offset:1},
  repeat: -1,
  yoyo: true,
  ease:Linear.easeNone});

TweenMax.fromTo("#stop2", 1.5, {
  attr:{offset:0}
}, {
  attr:{offset:2},
  repeat: -1,
  yoyo: true,
  ease:Linear.easeNone});
```

and this SVG:

```
<svg width="500"
    height="200"
    xmlns="http://www.w3.org/2000/svg"
    xmlns:xlink="http://www.w3.org/1999/xlink">
  <defs>
    <linearGradient id="Gradient">
      <stop id="stop1" offset="0" stop-color="white"
        stop-opacity="0" />
      <stop id="stop2" offset="0.3" stop-color="white"
        stop-opacity="1" />
    </linearGradient>
    <mask id="Mask">
      <rect x="0" y="0" width="500" height="200"
        fill="url(#Gradient)"  />
    </mask>
  </defs>

  <rect x="0" y="0" width="500" height="200" fill="#480048" />
  <rect x="0" y="0" width="500" height="200" fill="#C04848"
    mask="url(#Mask)" />
</svg>
```

Here, we're essentially creating a mask that uses a gradient to define its opacity and then moving the offset, which creates a pretty performant gradient animation. If you compare this to a background gradient animation, it performs much better because there aren't as many repaints.

We can also animate things like filters, which can be updated by interpolating the stdDeviation. In this pen (*http://codepen.io/sdras/pen/gaxGBB*), I'm looping through path points with MorphSVG and also updating the stdDeviation of a blur filter to create a flame that ebbs and flows, and has natural-looking movement (Figure 15-2).

Figure 15-2. If you animate things like filters, you can get unstable movement, which is great for elements of nature, like flame

Here's the relevant part of the code:

```
function flame() {
  var tl = new TimelineMax();

  tl.add("begin");
  tl.fromTo(blurNode, 2.5, {
    attr: {
      stdDeviation: 9
    }
  }, {
    attr: {
      stdDeviation: 3
    }
  }, "begin");
  var num = 9;
  for (var i = 1; i <= num; i++) {
    tl.to(fStable, 1, {
      morphSVG: {
        shape: "#f" + i
      },
      opacity: ((Math.random() * 0.7) + 0.7),
      ease: Linear.easeNone
    }, "begin+=" + i);
```

```
    }
    ...

    return tl;
}
```

Practical Application: Animating the viewBox

Controlling the way that a data visualization lays out on your page on the fly is a powerful way to convey information. In the past, we've talked about how we can use this to hide and show information (*http://bit.ly/2mHuDKn*) for responsive development. When working with SVG, we can do this by using the `viewBox` as a camera, isolating the relevant information on the page to highlight information for the viewer. There are many uses for this technique. We're going to look at a new way of working with it dynamically to get the processor to do the heavy lifting for us.

Before we go into animating the `viewBox`, we should discuss what the `viewBox` in SVG *is*. I'm just going to cover the basics here, but if you want a deep dive, there are some great articles (*http://bit.ly/2mpCcJo*) to help with that (*http://bit.ly/2mB09KS*).

The `viewBox` acts as a *window* through which you see into your SVG. It's defined with four coordinate values: `min-x`, `min-y`, `width`, and `height`. You can see the full drawing (*http://bit.ly/2iw6sxH*) in Figure 15-3.

Figure 15-3. The full SVG

The black box around it is defining the `viewBox`. If you're familiar with Illustrator, this is the artboard. You can change up the artboard in Illustrator by going to File →

Document Setup → Edit Artboards. You can then crop your image on the fly and change the visible area. If you know that your graphic is exactly the size of your desired viewBox, you can do this quickly with Object → Artboards → Fit to Artwork Bounds.

When we keep the viewBox the same, and we can change the width and height of the SVG (*http://bit.ly/2hKDvRl*).

You can think about it a little like the SVG DOM plotting itself along a grid. That grid can shrink and grow, but the aspect ratio of the grid stays consistent. In Figure 15-4 we have the SVG plotted at 0 min of the x-axis of the grid and 0 min of the y-axis. The width expands across by 384.5 and the height by 250, roughly.

Figure 15-4. The coordinates of the original viewBox

If we group those houses together, we can see where they lie as well (Figure 15-5).

Figure 15-5. The coordinates, and therefore, viewBox of a group within the graphic

We can crop the whole visible area to just the houses by changing the viewBox to "215 160 42.2 20".

In order to find the viewBox coordinates for that group, we could do some measuring, editing by hand, but that's pretty arduous and, because the viewBox is scalable, gets tricky. Luckily for us, there's a native method we can use called getBBox() (*https://www.w3.org/TR/SVG/types.html*). This returns the bounding box at the time that the method is called, and is exclusive of stroke, masking, or filter effects. It returns an SVGRect (*http://bit.ly/2mpC6lf*) object at the time that it's called (even if it hasn't yet been rendered).

The cool thing about the SVGRect object is that it returns four values: the x-min, y-min, width, and height (Figure 15-6). Sounds a bit familiar, huh?

```
▼ SVGRect 🗎
    height: 19.600006103515625
    width: 42.199981689453125
    x: 215.10000610351562
    y: 160
  ▶ __proto__: SVGRect
```

Figure 15-6. The SVGRect object

This is really handy for us, because it means in order to update the viewBox dynamically all we have to do is store the values from the object as our new viewBox string, like so:

```
var newView = "" + hb.x + " " + hb.y + " " + hb.width + " " + hb.height;
```

If you're using ES6 template literals, you can make this much more legible:

```
const newView = `${hb.x} ${hb.y} ${hb.width} ${hb.height}`;
```

We can then set the new `viewBox` string as the `viewBox` attribute on the SVG:

```
const houses = document.getElementById("houses");
const hb = houses.getBBox();

// check the console for the SVGRect object
console.log(hb);

// we store the values from the object as our new viewBox string
const newView = `${hb.x} ${hb.y} ${hb.width} ${hb.height}`;

// we then set the new viewBox string as the viewBox attribute on the SVG
const foo = document.getElementById("foo");
foo.setAttribute("viewBox", newView);
```

Now we're cooking with gas (see Figure 15-7).

Figure 15-7. The new, updated viewBox, set by the SVGRect object

To animate to the new `viewBox` values, we have a few options, all using JavaScript (for the time being):

- We can use `requestAnimationFrame()` (*http://bit.ly/2lkN4nc*) with a polyfill to update the values of our coordinates over time.
- We can use GreenSock's AttrPlugin (bundled with TweenMax) to animate it.
- We can use React-Motion to update the attributes on a click event.

The cool thing about GreenSock is it can animate any two integers, so it's a pretty nice tool for this. I'm going to use GreenSock in the following example because there are a number of other things I want to animate, and I'd like quick, finite control of my easing values, but the other methods would work as well.

VGRect Returns a Rectangle

One thing to keep in mind is that SVGRect will always return a rectangle, even if the element in question is not one, and there are no diagonals, even when it's transformed. The bounding box you see is what you get when you take the original bounding box of the circle, transform it, then find the bounding box for that diagonal box in the parent coordinate system. That's why the boxes are sometimes much larger than the shapes.

Figure 15-8 and its corresponding demo (*http://codepen.io/sdras/pen/MwxRBL*) show some rotating shapes with a stroke applied so that you can see what I mean.

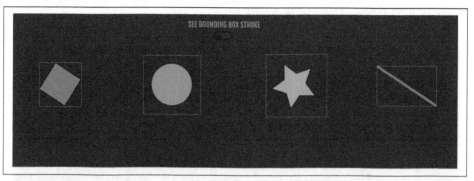

Figure 15-8. When an SVG element is transformed, the bounding box doesn't go with it —there are no diagonals; the box expands and creates a rectangle, even with circles and lines

In Figures 15-9 and 15-10 and their corresponding demo (*http://codepen.io/ sdras/pen/dXoLEJ*), I have a map, and when users interact with it, I want to give more information on the specific country they select.

Figure 15-9. The Crime Statistics map with hotspots

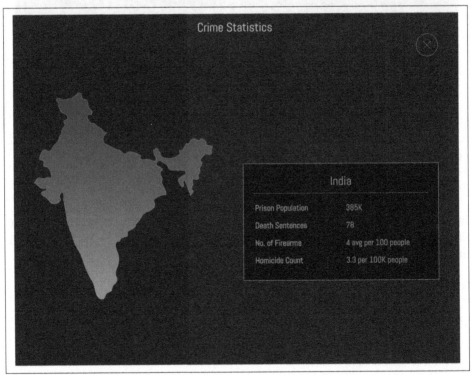

Figure 15-10. The expanded view, with India zoomed in by adjusting the viewBox

I have a repeated animation for the hotspots. I'm also using some simple data attributes on the elements themselves so that I can store and use that information to animate. Consistent naming is important here; it's how I'm controlling which country is expanded and what details are shown:

```
<g data-name="usa" class="hotspot">
  <circle id="dot2" cx="221" cy="249" r="2.4" fill="url(#radial-gradient)"/>
  <circle id="dot1" cx="221" cy="249" r="2.4" fill="url(#radial-gradient)"/>
  <circle id="dotmid" cx="221" cy="249" r="2.3" fill="#45c6db"/>
</g>
```

I've also added some extra padding to the hotspot elements so that their click target is large enough for mobile devices and our fingers:

```
.hotspot {
  cursor: pointer;
  /* make the hit targets bigger for mobile */
  padding: 20px;
}
```

I can then write a function that, on click, passes in the data attribute and updates the viewBox based on the shape of the country. I've added 200 to the width to accommodate the text beside the country:

```
// interaction
function zoomIn(country) {
// zooming in part
var currentCountry = document.getElementById(country),
    s = currentCountry.getBBox(),
    newView = "" + s.x + " " + s.y + " " + (s.width + 200) + " " + s.height,
    group1 = [".text-" + country, ".x-out"],
    tl = new TimelineMax();

    tl.add("zIn");
    tl.fromTo(map, 1.5, {
      attr: { viewBox: "0 0 1795.2 875.1"}
    }, {
      attr: { viewBox: newView }
    }, "zIn");
    tl.to(".text-" + country, 0.1, {
      display: "block"
    }, "zIn");
    tl.fromTo(group2, 0.25, {
      opacity: 1
    }, {
      opacity: 0,
      ease: Circ.easeIn
    }, "zIn");
    tl.fromTo(currentCountry, 0.35, {
      opacity: 0
    }, {
      opacity: 1,
```

```
      ease: Circ.easeOut
    }, "zIn+=0.5");
    tl.fromTo(group1, 0.5, {
      opacity: 0
    }, {
      opacity: 0.65,
      ease: Sine.easeOut
    }, "zIn+=1");
}

$(".hotspot").on("click", function() {
  var area = this.getAttribute('data-name');
  $(".x-out").attr("data-info", area);
  zoomIn(area);
});
```

If I wanted my code to be super slim, I could have wrapped the timeline in a function and simply reversed it when someone clicked the ×, but when I tried that, the animation was just a little sloppier than I liked, so I created a new function to refine the timing a little. I could also have used `tl.to` instead of `.fromTo`, but I've found that when restarting animations, offering an initial value in `.fromTo` helps to stabilize it a bit (particularly if you don't know who might be updating your code).

I used jQuery in this example instead of vanilla JavaScript, so if you find my body later, you know the motive.

viewBox in CSS?

A proposal has been made to make `viewBox` a CSS property (*http://bit.ly/2lvheVD*), which I heavily support. If you want to support it too, please either add a comment with technical feedback or add a thumbs up to one of the existing comments (to avoid crowding the main thread). A CSS property to control the `viewBox` would be wonderful, because we could easily apply media queries and animation, perhaps even reducing the layout triggers and repaints required for such updates.

Another Demo: A Guided Infographic

For extra fun, I made a small flowchart (*http://codepen.io/sdras/full/VjvGJM/*) to show how this technique can be used to guide users. This particular chart guides users toward choosing the right image format for the job (Figure 15-11).

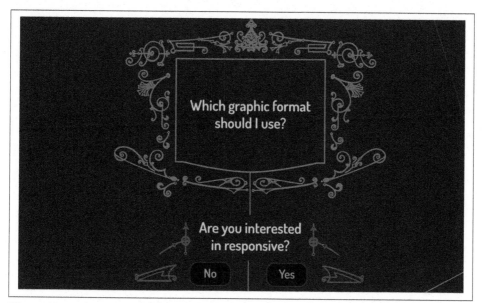

Figure 15-11. An animated flowchart using the viewBox and getBBox() for dynamic updates

Animation warning: It's potentially dizzying, so don't play with it if you have a vestibular disorder. If I embedded this on a production site I might have a toggle to turn the animation off or a fallback to a simplified questionnaire.

CHAPTER 16

Responsive Animation

Animation on the web is particularly nuanced, as we have to adjust our work to take into account bandwidth, code compatibility, and product design. In this chapter we'll go over some techniques for creating a truly responsive scalable animation. We'll also cover different ways of working with the animation to achieve positive user experiences and parity across our multidevice world.

Some Quick Responsive Tips

At the very least we should ensure that interaction also works well on mobile, but if we'd like to create interactions that take advantage of all of the gestures mobile has to offer, we can use libraries like ZingTouch (*http://bit.ly/2m9t2Av*) or Hammer.js (*http://hammerjs.github.io/*) to work with swipe or multiple finger detection. With a bit of work, these interactions can all be created through native detection as well.

Responsive web pages can specify `initial-scale=1.0` in the `<meta>` tag so that the device does not wait the default 300 ms for a second tap before calling the action. Interactions for touch events must either start from a larger touch target (40×40 px or greater) or use `@media(pointer:coarse)`, as support allows.

GreenSock and Responsive SVG

The number-one reason I use GSAP has to do with cross-browser support for SVG transforms. Stable SVG rotation is very cumbersome (*http://bit.ly/2lktYgW*). In almost every browser, `transform-origin` problems persist, and they are completely unsupported in IE. This problem is clearly exacerbated when attempting to use transforms in a responsive manner, as any small `transform-origin` anomalies are exaggerated and difficult to override.

Not only does GreenSock correct this behavior, but with support back to IE9, it offers a few more tools that make responsive design and development particularly solid. Currently, transforms on SVG elements with native rendering technologies (and subsequently, other JS libraries that use them) do not support correct rendering based on percentages. GSAP solves this issue with matrix calculations.

Let's first establish that by removing the width and height values from the SVG itself, defining the `viewBox`, and then using CSS or JS to control the width and height of the SVG, we can easily make an SVG adjust to any kind of responsive implementation. You can also add `preserveAspectRatio="xMinYMin meet"` to ensure that all corresponding dimensions will scale appropriately and respective to one another, but since that's the default, it's not strictly necessary. There's a great playground (*http://bit.ly/2lNbuJv*) by Sara Soueidan if you'd like to get more background on the `viewBox` and scaling.

There are three other particular strengths that GSAP with respect to SVG, all employing the use of transforms. The first is that aside from `transformOrigin`, GSAP now has built-in support for `svgOrigin`. This means that you can choose whether you want your element to transform based on the element itself (i.e., rotating on its own axis) or using a coordinate in the SVG `viewBox`. With `svgOrigin`, you declare values according to the `viewBox` coordinates. In other words, if your `viewBox` is `"0 0 400 400"` and you want to spin around the SVG's center, you would declare `svgOrigin: "200 200"`. Usually you will find that moving and adjusting a `transformOrigin` is enough. But in the case of Figure 16-1 and its corresponding pen (*http://codepen.io/sdras/pen/doZReX*), I made a cow spin around the moon at a certain part of the `viewBox`, and because I used an `svgOrigin` coordinate it was very easy to make this animation responsive, spinning on one solid coordinate that's stable no matter what size the SVG is:

```
TweenMax.set(cow, {
  svgOrigin:"321.05, 323.3",
  rotation:50
});
```

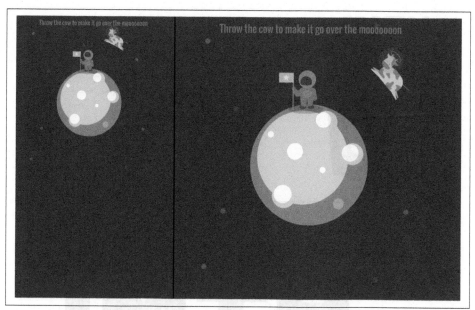

Figure 16-1. This SVG animation is draggable and pivots on a single point inside the SVG viewBox with svgOrigin, so it's completely stable across responsive implementations (size the window down horizontally to watch the animation adjust to the viewport)

The next great feature we'll cover is `smoothOrigin` on SVG elements. Typically, if you change the transform origin on elements after they've already been transformed, the movement becomes complex and counterintuitive, as seen in Figure 16-2 and its corresponding pen (*http://codepen.io/1Marc/full/DCvFm*).

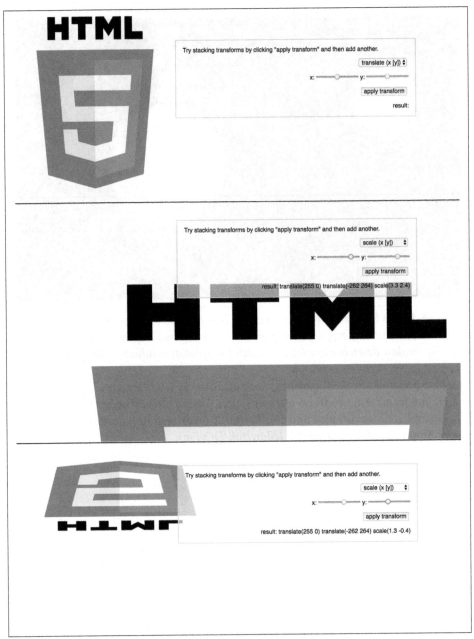

Figure 16-2. A pen showing that the spec's interpretation of how stacking transforms behave is counterintuitive (courtesy of Marc Grabinski)

As explained in a video by Carl Schooff of GreenSock (*http://bit.ly/2mpuEXo*), smoothOrigin corrects for this problem. It makes sure that when you change the transform origin for an SVG element and subsequently move it again, it doesn't cause any kind of strange jumpiness (which is what the spec will interpret).

This resolves a huge amount of counterintuitive and hair-pulling behavior when working with a longer and more complex responsive animation. GSAP also leaves you the option of turning this off with one line of code, in the edge case that you'd like to use the native rendering: `CSSPlugin.defaultSmoothOrigin = false;`.

The last great feature for complex responsive animations in GSAP is the ability to do percentage-based animations dependent on the SVG elements themselves. CSS and SMIL don't have good support for this type of behavior. Just like with the BezierPlugin, GSAP offers the most backward compatibility and cross-browser support for percentage-based SVG transforms. Check out Figure 16-3, a pen courtesy of Green-Sock:

```
var playBtn = document.getElementById("play"),
    tl = new TimelineMax({repeat:1, yoyo:true, paused:true});

tl.staggerTo(".box", 0.5, {x:"100%"}, 0.4)

play.onclick = function() {
  tl.restart();
}
```

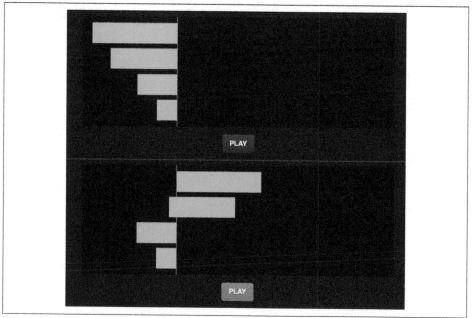

Figure 16-3. GreenSock allows you to do percentage-based transforms on SVG elements, which is a really nice feature for responsive development

Responsive SVG, with or without GreenSock

Percentage-based transforms on SVG elements are really impressive and useful. In responsive development, we make good use of flexbox, percentages, and units that allow us to scale or expand to fit containers. But even more amazing when you move to SVG *is the fact that you might not need them.* SVG transforms rely on the SVG canvas, not absolute, browser window–defined pixel integers. We're moving our elements according to the SVG DOM. And elements aren't the only thing that's scalable. *All of the corresponding transforms and movements are as well.*

There are no media queries to be found. We move things based on the x- and y-axes, like so:

```
tl.staggerFromTo($iPop, 0.3, {
  scale: 0,
  x: 0,
  y: 0
}, {
  scale: 1,
  x: 30,
  y: -30,
  ease: Back.easeOut
}, 0.1, "start+=0.3")
```

Figure 16-4 and its corresponding demo (*http://codepen.io/sdras/full/jPLgQM/*) show the result.

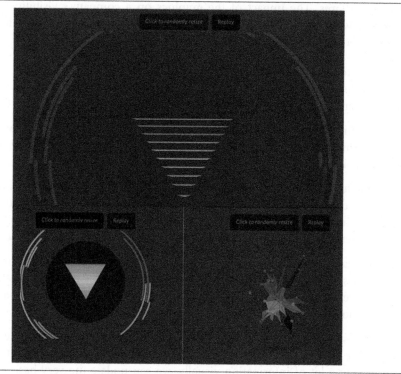

Figure 16-4. The animation changes size when you click the button, but the animation experience stays consistent

Note that we're not moving things with percentage-based transforms. Our animation is establishing behavior based on the `viewBox`, and therefore, responsive development becomes as easy as removing the width and height and declaring it elsewhere.

It's nice to just "squish" an animation to fit our viewport, but we all know that true responsive development is a more involved process than that. Let's take our new shiny tools and couple them with some responsive development, from start to finish.

There are a few ways we can do this. One is to take a large SVG sprite and shift the `viewBox` with a media query event handler (*http://bit.ly/2lYYYH3*).

Responsive Reorganization by Updating the ViewBox

Do you remember when people used to use infographics? Infographics became very popular because of their impact on conversion. On the user side, they were full of quick, easy-to-digest information. They were colorful, and when created well, clearly illustrated comparative information that one could pick up at a glance. On the creator's side, they increased the ROI (*http://bit.ly/2lhds0Y*) (return on investment) of posts and shares. The impact of the graphics on a company's visibility and brand awareness was staggering (*http://bit.ly/2mDH3Tq*). The Whole Brain Blog boasted numbers (*http://bit.ly/2lN4nkk*) such as:

- Traffic to the website increased by *over 400%*
- Leads increased by *almost 4,500%*
- Number of new visitors to the site increased by *almost 78%*

But one thing all of these posts have in common is that they are *at least two years old*. If infographics have that kind of potential for performance, why do they seem to be considered a played out fad?

One possible reason is the tipping point for mobile (*http://bit.ly/2m3Jth6*). Infographics that are exciting and all-encompassing on the desktop become an arduous pinch-n-grab affair on a mobile device. With the rise of mobile traffic, sharing via social media causes frustration and a decline of the engagement potential of these images.

The next reason is a little simpler. When a concept doesn't adjust to the present context, it fades away. With more interactivity and motion on the web, a static graphic doesn't have the same pull as something that is more visually exciting, and here is where motion trumps all.

Animation shouldn't be considered at the end of the design and development process; it should be the bones (*http://bit.ly/2lhdplV*). If we marry that idea with the concept of conveying a lot of information visually, we can update the very basis of what an infographic is and does. I took the text content of an infographic I found in David McCandless's book *Knowledge Is Beautiful* (Harper Design) and reimagined the look, feel, and implementation to create a responsive, animated infographic.

Please view the full pen (*http://codepen.io/sdras/full/JdJgrB/*) that corresponds to Figure 16-5, as the embedded pen shows the collapsed view. Keep in mind that the progress of the text transitions is sped up here in order to demonstrate the animation, not necessarily the content.

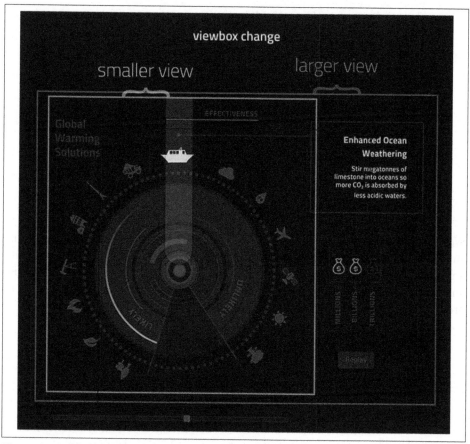

Figure 16-5. The viewBox shifts for mobile and desktop views of the infographic

In terms of design, traditional infographics typically make use of a salon-style, visually loaded method. Here, we've still filled the usable image area but updated the design to feel a little more clean. We didn't overload the graphic with many elements, because unlike with traditional static infographics, if there are too many different moving parts it's disorienting for the viewer. It's also heavier to load, so there is a performance hit.

In terms of responsive design, instead of having the entire presentation be fluid throughout, we had the infographic stay in place until a breakpoint, and then moved elements to different positions, allowing the main SVG to respond fluidly at that juncture. Even though we designed desktop-first, our media queries are a mobile-first implementation. I used an SVG that is very easy to make fluid, adjusting the viewport slightly on mobile with JavaScript:

```
var shape = document.getElementById("svg");

// media query event handler
if (matchMedia) {
  var mq = window.matchMedia("(min-width: 826px)");
  mq.addListener(WidthChange);
  WidthChange(mq);
}
// media query change
function WidthChange(mq) {
  if (mq.matches) {
    shape.setAttribute("viewBox", "0 0 765 587");
  } else {
    shape.setAttribute("viewBox", "0 0 592 588");
  }
};
```

We're then animating it with GreenSock to take advantage of the both the timeline and the ability to scrub the animation to find different points in time to interact with on a slider. Here is an example of one piece of information in the graphic displaying on the timeline. Note that we've added a relative time for all of these animations to fire at using a label:

```
tl.add("likely");
tl.to($(".p1"), 0.3, {
    scale: 1.3,
    transformOrigin: "50% 100%",
    fill: $blue,
    ease: Bounce.easeOut
}, "likely")
.to($effect, 0.3, {
   y: -10,
   ease: Circ.easeOut
}, "likely")
.to($eLine, 0.3, {
  stroke: $orange,
  ease: Sine.easeOut
}, "likely")
.fromTo($(".d1"), 0.3, {
  opacity: 0,
  scale: 0.7
}, {
  opacity: 1,
  scale: 1,
  ease: Back.easeOut
}, "likely")
.to($m1, 0.3, {
   fill: $green,
   ease: Circ.easeOut
}, "likely");
```

We can improve the accessibility of the graphic by adding a `<title>` element. You can also supply an `aria-labelledby` attribute in the `<svg>` element to reinforce the relationship between these two elements:

```
<svg aria-labelledby="title" id="svg" xmlns="http://www.w3.org/2000/svg"
    viewBox="0 0 765 587">
  <title id="title" lang="en">Circle of icons that illustrate Global Warming
    Solutions</title>
```

If you need to, you can supply a title for any element in the SVG DOM. You can find more information on implementation in a great article by Dudley Storey (*http://bit.ly/2lrOtZR*). In the case of this demo, we kept the text separate so that it's still completely legible to screen readers. This is an improvement over the original infographics, which, as static images, could not be accessed in this way.

This demo is merely a sketch, to ponder methods by which we can give shareable information more muscle with responsive animation. The same thing could also be achieved with PNGs, CSS, canvas, and variety of other methods. The potential that we have with the tools now supported on the web is exciting, and they can breathe new life into older concepts.

Responsive Reorganization with Multiple SVGs and Media Queries

We covered one solution for this in detail in Chapter 3. Another is to *design our animation using interlocking parts*, much like Tetris pieces, and use multiple SVGs that can be reconfigured. Let's explore the latter, as shown in Figure 16-6 and its corresponding pen (*http://codepen.io/sdras/full/waXKPw/*).

Figure 16-6. An interactive Huggy Laser Panda Factory

In the Huggy Laser Panda Factory pen, there are three distinct parts to the factory. In order to keep our code organized, each section can accept one type of user interaction, which then triggers its own timeline (Figure 16-7).

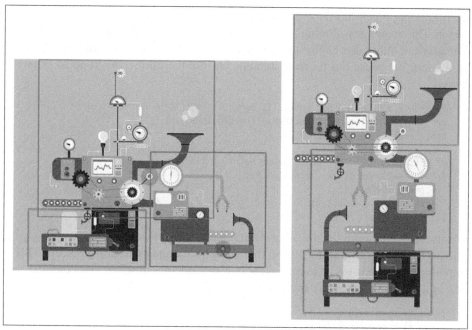

Figure 16-7. Each one of the SVGs interlocks and reconfigures, depending on the viewport size

Keeping the inline SVGs distinct from one another also allows us to collapse them and move them according to percentages or integers on variable viewports, making our animation flexible for both mobile and future iterations. We've plotted out an initial view for desktop, as well as how it will be reconfigured for smaller displays, including a `transform: scaleX(-1);` line to reflect the second portion on mobile so it will fit gracefully, with a mobile-first implementation:

```
@media (max-width: 730px) {
  .second {
    width: 70%;
    top: -90px;
    margin-left: 70px;
    transform: scaleX(-1);
  }
}


@media (min-width: 731px) {
  .second {
    width: 350px;
    margin-left: 365px;
    top: 370px !important;
  }
}
```

Each building block has its own function, named for what part of the animation it serves. This avoids any scoping problems and keeps everything organized and legible. The user can only trigger behaviors relative to the same SVG, or building block, of the animation. We pause the timeline initially, but use the button or group to restart it here:

```
// create a timeline but initially pause it so that we can control it via click
var triggerPaint = new TimelineMax({paused:true});
triggerPaint.add(paintPanda());

// this button kicks off the panda painting timeline
$("#button").on("click", function(e){
  e.preventDefault();
  triggerPaint.restart();
});
```

We also have a looping timeline that covers many elements in the document. We set a relative label to the beginning of it so that we can set loops on multiple objects. This is important because if we let loops follow one another in a timeline, only the first will fire, as it will run forever and the second one will wait to follow indefinitely:

```
function revolve() {
  var tl = new TimelineMax();

  tl.add("begin");
  tl.to(gear, 4, {
  transformOrigin:"50% 50%",
  rotation:360,
  repeat:-1,
  ease: Linear.easeNone
}, "begin");
  tl.to(wind, 2, {
  transformOrigin:"50% 50%",
  rotation:360,
  repeat:-1,
  ease: Linear.easeNone
}, "begin");

  // ...
  return tl;
}

var repeat = new TimelineMax();
repeat.add(revolve());
```

We now have four timelines in total: three that are cleanly associated with each section, and the global looping timeline. Our interaction and animations scale with each individual SVG, so we are free to move and adjust them in the configurations that we like for different viewports, and the code stays direct and organized.

Less Pizzazz on Mobile

Let's face it, mobile connections (particularly in less-developed countries) can be pretty slow. Whether you only have a few key animation interactions on your site or a huge WebGL experience, sometimes an animation that looks beautiful on desktop need not scale down to a mobile experience.

In the case of a large canvas animation, or even a really complex SVG animation that is not critical to the user experience, sometimes the best thing you can do is to tone it down or turn it off for smaller devices.

Active Theory's site does a beautiful job of this (see Figure 16-8) by showing you a full particle canvas animation on desktop, which is replaced with a simple polygon background on mobile. The interactions on mobile are still very on-point, transitioning beautifully beyond even what we expect on native.

Figure 16-8. Active Theory keeps its visual language consistent, while dropping heavy canvas animations on mobile

The team still shows off its interaction prowess in the way you navigate the site, which is arguably more impressive on mobile than an animated background would be anyway. The design saves the bandwidth for what counts.

Have a Plan

Whether you design for responsiveness from start to finish or simply turn animations off on mobile, having a concrete plan for what your viewers experience from device to device is vital. This is particularly true in a landscape where mobile is king. Content, type of image, and user bandwidth should all help guide animation choices for responsive design.

CHAPTER 17

Designing, Prototyping, and Animation in Component Libraries

Our modern frontend workflow has matured over time to include design systems and component libraries that help us stay organized, improve workflows, and simplify maintenance. These systems, when executed well, ensure proper documentation of the code available and enable our systems to scale with reduced communication conflicts.

But while most of these systems take a critical stance on fonts, colors, and general building blocks, their treatment of animation remains disorganized and ad hoc. Fortunately, we can leverage existing structures and workflows to reduce friction when it comes to animation and create cohesive and performant user experiences.

In this chapter, we'll break down how to design, plan, and implement animations.

Designing an Animation

Animations, like any other facet of the web, must be designed. You can refer to the following articles on Smashing Magazine (*https://www.smashingmagazine.com*) for details as to why:

- "Functional Animation in UX Design" (*http://bit.ly/2mx04bd*), by Amit Daliot
- "The State of Animation 2014" (*http://bit.ly/2l5zpVC*), by Rachel Nabors
- "The Guide to CSS Animation: Principles and Examples" (*http://bit.ly/2mDBHHY*), by Tom Waterhouse

As web developers, we think about the effects of typography, layout, interaction, and shifting viewports, but when incorporating animation we have another factor to consider: time.

It's not just an extra aspect to consider, either: it increases the complexity of each of the aforementioned parameters exponentially. But rather than viewing this as a heavy mass of ideas, we can bake animation into the core of our user experience process to create dazzling, exciting, and engaging work that pushes boundaries and collectively elevates the medium of the web.

Working with the Language of Motion

Everyone has different ways of working and nothing is gospel, but here are a few key points that I have discovered after working at this for a while.

First, pay attention to how stuff moves. This one might make you laugh, it's so simple. But how often do you really watch water pour into a glass? What makes one person's gait so recognizable?

Most people start with a ball bouncing, and that's a great exercise, partly because the simplicity can show you character, weight, and dynamism. Figure 17-1 and its corresponding demo (*http://codepen.io/sdras/pen/zxJWBJ*) show two balls bouncing: can you guess which is hard and which is soft?

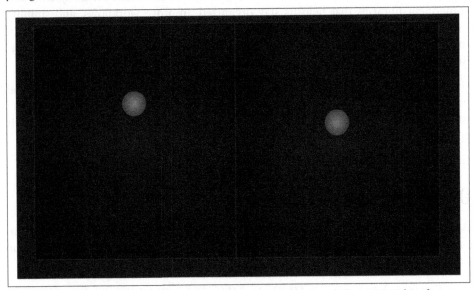

Figure 17-1. You can tell the difference in "character"—how soft the material is, for instance—even though both balls are bouncing at the same rate

How do you know which is which? First, there is the elasticity of the objects. One stays consistently round; the other is manipulated based on the impact. What else? Well, there's the movement: one seems fairly rigid, and the other is more playful. Though they have the same timing, their physical motions imply different masses. Easing functions convey the density of the object.

Note also that even though they have the same timing, the easing function is used in such a way that they have different keyframes. If I placed a strobe light on these balls, you would see them at different places during the same time period. This concept has a term in old cel animation: *spacing*. See Figure 17-2 and its corresponding demo (*http://codepen.io/sdras/pen/MYdQor*).

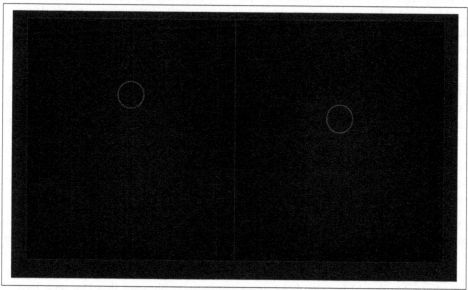

Figure 17-2. By showing the outline, we can see the "spacing" and the difference between each

This can also come in the form of the motion of secondary elements. If someone shakes a glass, how is the water inside affected? When someone kicks a rock, how does the rock express the force of impact? There's a great example of elemental motion design available on Dribbble.com (*http://bit.ly/2l8r97e*).

As Hans Bacher discusses in *Dream Worlds* (Focal Press), when animators were working on *Beauty and the Beast* they were flown to London and France to observe the styles of these places. You might not have this kind of budget (but if you do, take me with you!); luckily, the internet has plenty of visual, historical, and spatial information for you to work from.

Follow your interests. If you have any leeway at all in the content of the animation, use that to your advantage. Genuine interest and enthusiasm are easily conveyed. You're more likely to follow a project through if the content excites you.

Rein It In

Unlike fonts, colors, and so on, we tend to add animation in as a last step, which leads to disorganized implementations that lack overall cohesion. If you asked a designer or developer to create a mockup or build a UI without knowing the fonts they were working with, they would dislike the idea. Not knowing the building blocks they're working with—leaving out something so fundamental at the start—means that the design can fall apart or the development can break. It's the same with good animation. Avoid the temptation to load up your design with flashy animations at the end; with animation, less is often more.

The first step in reining in your use of animation is to perform an animation audit. Look at all the places you are using animation on your site, or the places you aren't using animation but probably should be. (Hint: perceived performance of a loader on a form submission can dramatically change your bounce rates.)

Not sure how to perform a good audit? Val Head has a great chapter on it in her book *Designing Interface Animations* (Rosenfeld Media), which contains buckets of research and great ideas.

Even some beautiful component libraries that have animation in the docs make this mistake. *You don't need every kind of animation, just like you don't need every kind of font.* Having too many options bloats your code. Ask yourself questions like "Do I really need a flip 180 degree animation?" I can't even conceive of a place on a typical UI where that would be useful, yet most component libraries that I've seen have a mixin that does just this.

Which leads to...

Have an Opinion

Many people are confused about material design (*http://bit.ly/2lZ7MwV*). They think that material design *is* motion design, mostly because they've never seen anyone take a stance on animation before and document these opinions well. But every time you use material design as your motion design language, people look at your site and think GOOGLE. Now that's good branding.

By using Google's motion design language and not your own, you're losing out on a chance to be memorable on your own website.

The impact of Google's material design, in my mind, lies less with the design language itself, and more with that it was the first major industry example of a company incorporating animation guidelines in its branding. For the first time, people started thinking about the style of animation as a functioning entity that had a voice—one that must be designed in cohesion with everything else.

If your company is a well-trusted, stoic insurance company, the character of any animation on your site is going to be less flamboyant and more formal, and you'll tend to use linear eases rather than bounce or elastic motion. But with branding that's more comfortable and friendly, on a site like Zendesk's or MailChimp's, the form should follow the branding and accordingly have more lively animation, while still communicating effectively; something with the charm of Chris Gannon's loaders (*http://bit.ly/2lPaMK1*) is simple, yet exciting.

If you think back to the first time you cried because of a fictional character, it was likely animated. In Aarron Walters's *Designing for Emotion* (A Book Apart), he discusses how emotion is tied to the limbic system: we are more likely to remember something that becomes part of our emotional memory. Chapter 7 of his book goes into hard numbers on how much return on investment can be gained by focusing on the impact of users' emotive experiences.

If you have a static piece of content that looks like a Photoshop mock-up on a web page, the viewer engagement stops where your CSS does. Animation allows us to show rather than tell, a vital tactic considering users typically only scan body content (*http://bit.ly/1i6NkSX*). It allows customers to attach themselves to our UIs personally, for their needs to unfold before them. If done correctly, the potential for positive engagement is staggering.

What does having an opinion on motion look like in practice? It could mean you've decided that you never flip things and that your eases are always going to glide. In that instance, you would put your efforts toward finding an ease that looks like it glides and pulling out any `transform: scaleX(-1)` animations you find on your site. Across teams, everyone knows not to spend time mocking up flipping animations (even if they're working on an entirely different codebase), and to instead work on something that feels like it glides. You save time and don't have to communicate again and again to make things feel cohesive.

Elevate This

Animation has to be taught to live on its own as a substantial part of the development process. We can accomplish this in several ways:

- Animation has to be designed just as the rest of the page is: with mock-ups, color palettes, storyboards with wireframes, and its own composition.
- Your design process should follow the same logical structure as your code.
- Animation must move toward being informative, appealing to rationality and guiding users' attention.
- Animation should follow branding guidelines, be part of a living style guide, and appeal to users' emotions.

- We shouldn't reinvent the wheel. Animation has existed outside of the web for ages. (Yes, you can go watch *Toy Story* for "research" purposes.)

Because animation is so engaging, it's easy to overdo it, but not everything on the screen needs to be animated. You don't start a war with the secret weapon. Animation can be a way of signifying the end or beginning of something, as well as directing your attention. With animation that is purposeful and planned according to viewer engagement, performance budget, and branding, we can elevate the medium. Val Head discusses this very clearly when she writes about invisible animation (*http://bit.ly/2lP522O*). Good animation should not seem out of place, nor be an afterthought.

Check out Oleg Solomka's Bubble layout demo (*http://codepen.io/sol0mka/full/yNOage/*) (it's nice with the sound on): the animation is delightful enough to keep you engaged as you navigate, but gets out of your way while you're reading the content. Keep in mind that the purpose of these tutorials is to showcase a particular method; in the wild, the implementation can even be toned down slightly to accommodate a professional, yet engaging effect.

Prototyping

After design, the next step is planning.

Backward to Move Forward

Before you begin animating, you *must* storyboard. Storyboarding is a very important part of the process because it allows you to work modularly in your code, in scenes. It allows you to plan out timing. And it allows you to work backward: to draw something and then slowly unveil it.

A common misconception is that your storyboards have to look like polished comics. I think that's often why people don't want to make them: they're scared of drawing; they're scared that their work has to look perfect; they're scared of spending all of their creative energy in the planning process, and they just want to start working on the project. I understand this completely. To avoid all of it, I encourage you to forget the Platonic ideal of a storyboard.

I was a scientific illustrator for the Field Museum of Natural History (*http://www.fieldmuseum.org/*) and Stanford. I was a professor of painting at a college. Can I draw? You betcha. Figure 17-3 is what my storyboards look like.

Am I ashamed of this? Not in the slightest. That storyboard took me 45 seconds and allowed me to understand and edit up front what I was going to spend many days making. Without it, my workflow would have doubled. Storyboards exist behind the scenes and are for personal communication. I'm not saying you can't create beautiful standalone work like Rachel Nabors (*http://bit.ly/2lZ55v5*), just that you don't have to.

Figure 17-3. Ugly storyboards are really helpful

Let's revisit our discussion about user empathy. You can accomplish this with storyboarding all of a user's interaction, from beginning to end, as well. Consider the article "Story Map" (*http://bit.ly/2lPcPOm*) by James Buckhouse. A story map takes you through the entire experience of visiting your site and becoming a customer, from beginning to end. It's a storyboard with muscle, one where you see the whole picture of a user's visit and therefore can make purposeful decisions based on desired direction and outcome.

It's probably not new to hear about storyboards in animation: little comics that allow animators to break down tasks scene by scene. But did you know that there are also *color scripts*? Just as you design color and overall branding for your site, animators at Disney and other animation houses create color scripts that work well with the colors of their main characters and inform the scene. You should be doing this, too.

This means you should spend some time on Adobe Kuler (*https://color.adobe.com/*), crafting color swatches. It takes a small amount of time at the start, but saves buckets while you're working. We all know color is meaningful. Working with it is made so much easier in CSS with preprocessor variables; use them to your advantage.

Tools

First, let's develop our vocabulary around planning an animation, because there are differences in what's available and when you want to use each tool.

Thumbnails are small notes to yourself (Figure 17-4). They don't have to be legible at all—even to you. They should take a matter of seconds, and are extremely basic so that you can iterate quickly and throw out ideas without any time wasted.

Figure 17-4. Thumbnails are very sketchy notes to yourself that take seconds and can be thrown away

Storyboards are one step up in fidelity from thumbnails. They are slightly more discernible, but not by much (Figure 17-5). You could feasibly show them to another person and communicate with them, but they aren't appropriate for a presentation unless it's very casual. Even if they're sketchy, they are likely to show many scenes.

Figure 17-5. Storyboards are slightly more high-fidelity, but don't have to be full draw-ings; you can actually communicate an idea to others with a storyboard, even if it's not well drawn

Prototypes are moving versions of your proposed animation. In order to not build out the whole thing, you have a few courses of action. One is a low-fidelity prototype, with just basic shapes moving around to get the motion down (Figure 17-6). This is so that you don't have to build out or incorporate the whole site.

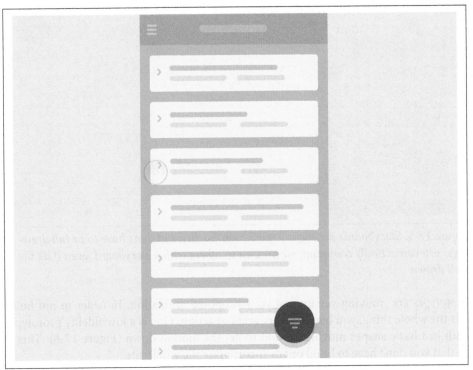

Figure 17-6. GIF mockup of basic UI shapes moving by Yaroslav Zubko

There's a great read (*http://bit.ly/2mnbuBr*) by Yaroslav Zubko about how to make prototypes with basic UI patterns and shapes. There's also a moving version of the GIF (*http://bit.ly/2jhdABm*).

Another way of working is to take a screenshot of the site or a flattened mockup and set it as a background image, absolutely positioning the elements that need to move on top of it and working with the motion. That way you can get up and running quickly with something that communicates to people in a presentation: it doesn't require much time, but it also looks pretty close to what it will eventually be. This can be good for stakeholder meetings.

There are also several very good tools for prototyping available if you're trying to collaborate between design and engineering, including:

- Principle (*http://principleformac.com/*)
- FramerJS (*https://framer.com/*)
- After Effects (*http://www.adobe.com/products/aftereffects.html*)
- Keynote (*http://www.apple.com/keynote/*)
- Straight-up code

Personally, I just go with straight code—I feel that some of these tools take time to learn that I'd rather devote to development practice. This has the added advantage that if one of your prototypes gets buy-in, you can clean up the code and use it in the actual codebase without having to rewrite anything or start over.

"Murder Your Darlings"

"Murder your darlings" is an old quotation traced back to Arthur Quiller-Couch (*http://bit.ly/2m3Mi1X*), but it's valid in design. Don't be afraid to remove or revise some of the aspects of your work that seem precious. You're never going to get things right the first time, so relax and make some mistakes. Whether you're a designer, a developer, or both, chances are you weren't as good in the beginning as you are now and it took a lot of ugly stuff in the middle to get to where you are. That's OK. This means trying different types of animation on for size, and messing all of those up, too. Did you learn JavaScript by only programming one kind of interaction using only one library? No. Did you learn to design only using one composition? I certainly hope not. The same principles apply to learning to animate as well.

Perhaps you can have both graphics editor and text editor open at the same time. You need to move fluidly back and forth between them. Don't be scared of retracing your steps, adding things, or editing. You will need ready access to your tooling for tasks like optimization (*http://bit.ly/2lPUOkp*), so you can move quickly through them. The further you put these things away from you, the lazier and sloppier you will become about adjusting, editing, and re-creating images or code as you need to. And you will need to.

You're going to have to redo your timing and easing a hundred times. Personally, I find it easiest when I'm using a tool like GreenSock's TimelineLite (*http://green sock.com/timelinelite*) to move pieces around. It lets you stack, stagger, overlap timings, and even animate full scenes

CSS is great for very small UI interactions; in fact, I really recommend it for those use cases because you don't need to load other resources. However, if you have more than two animations set on an object, you should probably consider switching over to GSAP. The ability to move a little forward or behind the last animation, or set them to fire at the same time no matter what, makes it too powerful a tool to avoid, particularly when you need to rehearse and readjust the timing. CSS makes you recalculate all of your values if something in your animation changes at the start, but the GSAP timeline does not.

This wouldn't be such a major issue if timing weren't so vital. Have you ever noticed how some comics have frames where there is no action? They create the illusion of a pause, and your brain treats it as such. Timing is vital for comedy, for whimsy, but also for UI animation that appears seamless or natural.

Just like in all design, the parts of an animation that look simple and effortless are sometimes the hardest to accomplish.

Design and Code Workflows

It's clear that storyboarding pays off in the design and planning stages of animations, but it can easily reap rewards in your code architecture, too. If your code reflects the same logical organization you use for your design, you gain all the benefits of clear, legible structure; and the more it mirrors the design process, the easier it is to share implementations between the two.

Functions should be named according to the scene you are in: even "sceneOne" will do. Similarly named variables look nice and neat, but they'll trip up you and your team in the long run, particularly as an animation gets more complex. Naming form elements as the characters they portray, and setting up your code in a clear way that mirrors your design, means less worrying about scoping problems, and more concrete divisions between JavaScript and Sass variables and assignments. It's also particularly helpful at the end when you have to go back in and adjust something: you will easily find your place again and know what follows.

Animations in Component Libraries

Sometimes people don't incorporate animation into a component library because they aren't sure how, beyond the base hover states. *All animation properties can be broken into interchangeable pieces.* This allows developers and designers alike to mix and match and iterate quickly, while still staying in the correct language. Here is a basic boilerplate structure (in Sass) for a basic set of CSS animation patterns (apologies for the length):

```
// ----   timing  ----//
$class-slug: t !default;

@for $i from 1 through 7 {
  .#{$class-slug}-#{$i} {
    animation-duration: 0.8 - (0.1s * $i);
  }
}

// ----   ease  ----//
$easein-quad: cubic-bezier(0.55, 0.085, 0.68, 0.53);
$easeout-quad: cubic-bezier(0.25, 0.46, 0.45, 0.94);
$easein-back: cubic-bezier(.57, .07, .6, 1.71);
$easeout-back: cubic-bezier(0.175, 0.885, 0.32, 1.275);

.entrance {
  animation-timing-function: $easeout-quad;
}
```

```scss
.entrance-emphasis {
  animation-timing-function: $easeout-back;
}
.exit {
  animation-timing-function: $easein-quad;
}
.exit-emphasis {
  animation-timing-function: $easein-back;
}

// ----   fill mode extend ---//
// we probably want this so we'll create a class that can be @extended as a
// default into our animations
.anim-fill-both {
  animation-fill-mode: both;
}

// animations
@keyframes pop {
  0% {
    transform: scale(0.9) translateZ(0);
  }
  100% {
    transform: scale(1) translateZ(0);
  }
}

.pop {
  animation-name: pop;
  @extend .anim-fill-both;
}

@keyframes unpop {
  0% {
    transform: scale(1) translateZ(0);
  }
  100% {
    transform: scale(0.9) translateZ(0);
  }
}

.unpop {
  animation-name: unpop;
  @extend .anim-fill-both;
}
```

You can also take a look at the full pen (*http://codepen.io/sdras/pen/qqVrxy*).

Create timing units, similar to h1, h2, h3. In a system I worked on recently, I called these t1, t2, t3, etc. t1 was reserved for longer pieces, while t5 was a bit like h5 in that it was the default (usually around .25 seconds or thereabouts). Keep animation easings for entrance, exit, entrance emphasis, and exit emphasis that people can commonly refer to. This, and the `animation-fill-mode`, are likely to be the only two properties that can be reused for the entrance and exit of the animation. Use the `animation-name` property to define the keyframes for the animation itself. I would recommend starting with five or six before making a slew of them, and see if you need more. Writing 30 different animations might seem like a nice resource, but just like with your color palette, having too many can bulk up your codebase unnecessarily and keep it from feeling cohesive. Think critically about what you need here.

The previous example is pared down, but you can see how in a robust system, having pieces that are interchangeable cached across the whole system would save time for iterations and prototyping, not to mention making it easy to make adjustments for different-feeling movement on the same animation easily.

One low-hanging fruit might be a loader that leads to a success dialog. On a big site, you might have that pattern many times, so writing up a component that does only that helps you move faster while also allowing you to really zoom in and focus on that pattern. You avoid throwing something together at the last minute, or using GIFs, which are really heavy and also look mushy on a Retina display. You can make singular pieces that look refined and are reusable.

React and Vue implementations are great for reusable components, as you can create a building block with a common animation pattern, and once created, it can be a resource for all. Remember to take advantage of things like props to allow for timing and easing adjustments like we have in the previous example!

Buy-in

Sometimes people don't create animation resources simply because it gets deprioritized. But design systems were also something we once had to fight for. At the CSS Dev Conf in 2016, Rachel Nabors (*http://rachelnabors.com/*) demonstrated how to plot out animation wants versus needs on a graph (reproduced with her permission) to help prioritize them (Figures 17-7 and 17-8).

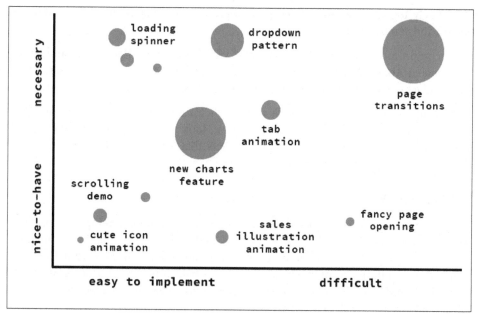

Figure 17-7. Wants versus needs (courtesy of Rachel Nabors)

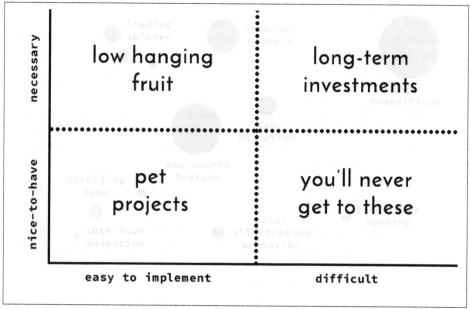

Figure 17-8. Level of difficulty in implementation (courtesy of Rachel Nabors)

This helps people you're working with figure out the relative necessity and workload of the addition of these animations and think more critically about it. You're also more likely to get something through if you're proving that what you're making is needed and can be reused.

Good compromises can be made this way: "We're not going to go all out and create an animated 'About Us' page like you wanted, but I suppose we can let our users know their contact email went through with a small progress and success notification."

Successfully pushing smaller projects through helps build trust with your team, and lets them see what this type of collaboration can look like. This builds up the type of relationship necessary to push through projects that are more involved. It can't be overstressed that good communication is key.

Time Is Money

Animation is often considered an afterthought in the corporate development process. We make mock-ups, pass them, develop them, and at the very end add an animation on top. Because of this, animated components can often look like what they are: whipped-cream fluff. It is only when animation is baked into the substance of layout, storyboard, and development processes that it holds meaning as a performant and substantial piece of a web experience.

Studios like Active Theory get away with engaging their clients with this conversation earlier in the design process because of their own branding: "We make bold things for the big guys." Clients who seek out Active Theory's work know they are paying for a blockbuster, knock-your-socks-off kind of web experience. This isn't going to be the case 98% of the time.

How do we change this? Again, the way that we usually do. In salesman's terms, that means "increase the ROI." In developer terms it means elevating the product to something that's useful, increases engagement, or has a positive experience, and then it won't be a waste of time or money. For more information on how to communicate with clients effectively, check out Mike Monteiro's books *You're My Favorite Client* or *Design Is a Job* (A Book Apart).

Before we gleefully skip into the sunset and make everything on the page move, we need to commit to some action items to make an effective change.

The first is communicating effectively with our clients. This does not mean railroading them into adhering to our beliefs. It means explaining the possible gains, assuring them we will A/B test (*http://bit.ly/2mDMZvS*) our interfaces and produce measurable results, and meeting them halfway on time allowances.

Consider the form we worked on earlier. Show your client prototypes of two forms—you can show them other people's work as an example if you don't have the time to build; CodePen has a great design patterns (*http://codepen.io/patterns*) resource. One form will present itself without feedback on the button or progress, or a snappy success UX; the other will incorporate all the lessons we've learned here. Or better yet, use A/B testing (usability testing with different variants) to prove the form with animation to be a more effective tool. Solid numbers are always better than subjective opinion, which can be shaped around trends, ignorance, or past bad experiences due to poor implementation.

Once you get the go-ahead, you can plan. You have performance budget allowances in new categories now:

- Time
- Experience
- Performance
- Color
- Composition
- User's time

This may seem overly complicated, but you should be able to give yourself basic ballpark figures within seconds for each of these, and they should be considered before you move on. Do you lack experience? Then you'll need a little more time, as with most things. Do you currently have a lot of other heavy assets on the page? You will need to be very careful loading up images, SVGs, scripts, and animation libraries. Does your site already have a very rich palette? You'll need to reuse those color variables.

The Sky's the Limit

Frank Thomas and Ollie Johnston's *Disney Animation: The Illusion of Life* (Disney Editions) begins with one of my all-time favorite quotes from Walt Disney: "Animation can explain whatever the mind of man can conceive." This quotation is so spot-on because it really is animation's strength: you can make anything happen. You can create and destroy worlds, excite or condemn.

That said, there is a lot to consider. Animation will never be more than empty calories if we don't design it the way we do other aspects of UX. As with our other tooling, it is a loss leader: we'll spend more time getting the variables and parameters set up at the start. But with that preparation, the character will tell us which road it would like to take during implementation, even if the character is a UI or branding.

Index

About the Author

Sarah Drasner is an award-winning speaker, consultant, and staff technical writer at CSS-Tricks. Sarah is also the cofounder of Web Animation Workshops, with Val Head. She's given a Frontend Masters workshop on Advanced SVG Animations, and was formerly manager of UX design and engineering at Trulia (Zillow). Sarah has won a number of awards, including CSS Dev Conf's "Best of the Best Award," as well as "Best Code Wrangler" from CSS Design Awards. She has worked for 15 years as a web developer and designer, and at points worked as a scientific illustrator and undergraduate professor and tutored a Byzantine icon painter in Santorini.

Colophon

The animal on the cover of *SVG Animations* is a Knysna turaco (*Tauraco corythaix*). It is part of the Musophagidae family (which translates to "banana-eaters"), and can be found in forests of South Africa and Swaziland.

The Knysna turaco is a distinguishable bird given its markings and coloring. Averaging 15 to 17 inches long (including their long tail), they are mostly green in plummage, which helps them blend in with treetops, but also have red flight feathers and shades of blue on the tops of their wings. Their bills are a bright orangish-red and come close to matching the color of their eye rings, which are lined with white borders along the bottom and part of the top of their eyes. Except for juveniles, their green crests are also topped with a streak of white.

Like other exotic birds, the Knysna turaco's diet relies heavily on insects and fruit, as well as earthworms. Food seems to be in great supply, so the Knysna turaco population is holding steady.

These birds build shallow nests in trees where breeding will take place. Breeding season varies based on region. One to two eggs are laid per cycle and are incubated for 12 to 21 days by both the male and female of a pair. It's not uncommon for just one of the two eggs to hatch. The young will venture outside of the nest after 18 days of hatching, but aren't mature and independent for an additional three weeks.

Many of the animals on O'Reilly covers are endangered; all of them are important to the world. To learn more about how you can help, go to *animals.oreilly.com*.

The cover illustration is by Karen Montgomery, based on a black and white engraving from *Wood's Illustrated Natural History*. The cover fonts are URW Typewriter and Guardian Sans. The text font is Adobe Minion Pro; the heading font is Adobe Myriad Condensed; and the code font is Dalton Maag's Ubuntu Mono.

Learn from experts.
Find the answers you need.

Sign up for a **10-day free trial** to get **unlimited access** to all of the content on Safari, including Learning Paths, interactive tutorials, and curated playlists that draw from thousands of ebooks and training videos on a wide range of topics, including data, design, DevOps, management, business—and much more.

Start your free trial at:

oreilly.com/safari

(No credit card required.)

Lightning Source UK Ltd.
Milton Keynes UK
UKOW07f1847260517
302082UK00001B/1/P